LOOKING *at* *leisure*

LOOKING *at*
leisure

DERRICK ANDERTON

Foreword by Neil Cossons,
Director of The Science Museum

Hodder & Stoughton

A MEMBER OF THE HODDER HEADLINE GROUP

British Library Cataloguing in Publication Data

Anderton, Derrick
  Looking at leisure
  I. Title
  790.0941

  ISBN 0-340-57041-5

First published 1992
Impression number   11 10 9 8 7 6 5 4 3 2
Year   1999   1998   1997   1996   1995   1994

Copyright © 1992 Derrick Anderton

Typeset by Wearset, Boldon, Tyne and Wear.
Printed in Great Britain for Hodder & Stoughton Educational, a division
of Hodder Headline PLC, 338 Euston Road, London NW1 3BH by
St Edmundsbury Press Limited, Bury St Edmunds, Suffolk.

Contents

Foreword

Neil Cossons

When we look back in a few hundred years' time at the history of the twentieth century, the emergence of the 'leisure economy' will be clearly visible as an era of rapid and cataclysmic global change. The social, economic and environmental impact of huge sectors of the world's population exercising freedom of choice in the spending of their disposable time and income will rank with population growth, famine and disease as one of the great issues that confront mankind. For while we have taken for granted that great works and proper regulation can bring public good in other areas of economic life and social activity, we are only now beginning to appreciate that the very quality of life we have sought to create for ourselves, through the generation of wealth – to provide people with time of their own and money to spend in that time – does in itself challenge the established order. Leisure and tourism – the two are not synonymous – can sustain whole national economies, redistribute wealth and generate environmental improvement. Equally, there are those who would argue that the 'leisure economy' exploits or destroys, through, for example, low wage levels or the detrimental effects on the landscape of too many people.

But although at first sight mass tourism as a major social and economic force may seem to be associated with the arrival of the motor car or the wide-bodied jet, its origins go back much further.

The seaside resort in its classic form was a creation of railway entrepreneurs, the Great Exhibition brought some six million people to London in the summer of 1851, and Thomas Cook's first tour – a pre-booked excursion train – ran just ten years before that.

Derrick Anderton traces the origins and subsequent progress of 'leisure' and looks with a perceptive eye at the many and peculiar contributions that this country has made to its pursuit, be it in the invention of a new ball game or through the way in which we handle the conservation of the landscape, for the purposes of public pleasure as much as anything else – through an intricate meshing of public authorities and voluntary bodies.

Looking at Leisure is, however, something that is more important than leisure reading: it provides an invaluable insight for both provider and consumer.

Neil Cossons
August 1991

1 The leisure revolution

Why do we talk of a leisure 'revolution'? Leisure has always been a necessary part of human life, and each generation has seen a significant but gradual increase in opportunities for the enjoyable use of leisure time. In certain periods, however, changes occur much more rapidly than in others, and during such times we can truly speak of 'revolution'. The period 1960–70 was a decade of rapid change: there were dramatic increases in the amounts of free time and money available to the average Briton. It has been said that all leisure is the product of surplus wealth. At all events, during the last twenty years, the provision of leisure facilities in this country – land-based and water-based, indoors and outdoors, physical and cultural, has expanded so rapidly that some writers have called it 'the leisure explosion'. We shall be looking at the many different recreational outlets which have been created to meet the demands of a population which has been given increasing amounts of free time, that is, *unoccupied* time when one can relax and pursue one's own pastimes. This time, when one is relieved of obligations and is given the chance to enjoy some sport or hobby to whatever level one is inclined or able, is valuable to the individual and to society.

In its syllabus for the Certificate for Recreation and Leisure Industries, the City and Guilds of London Institute give precise and useful definitions of some essential terms:

> *Leisure*: the time which allows the individual the opportunity to participate in any self-determined activity outside the recognized 'working time'. It may be play, recreation or sport; it may be active or passive.
>
> *Play*: a spontaneous response or activity undertaken for enjoyment, not necessarily controlled by predetermined guidelines, though it can be ordered by immediately agreed conventions.
>
> *Recreation*: any activity or pastime undertaken by the individual for enjoyment. It can encompass any activity participated in by the individual outside that period of the day recognized as 'working time'.
>
> *Sport*: any activity normally with an element of competitiveness undertaken within accepted or agreed rules, regulations or conventions, where success may well depend on physical ability.

The impact of tourism

Usually, leisure time is spent in a social setting whether it is in the company of friends with similar interests or at home in the company of family. The most important thing is that it should be literally 're-creative' in that it should provide us with the psychological resources and the physical well-being to help us continue with the business of earning a living or taking our place in the life of the community.

Travel and tourism especially in the form of the package tour holiday to a Continental destination, have probably done more than anything else to introduce the British public to a wider and more 'exotic' range of leisure pursuits. In favourable climates and picturesque natural settings, holiday-makers have had the opportunity to try their hands at water-skiing, dinghy sailing, scuba-diving, windsurfing and para-sailing. They have become accustomed to

Windsurfing is a popular sport to try on holiday.

warm, clean, freshwater pools in which to swim and dive. In some resorts they have experienced the full impact of a purpose-built leisure complex situated in an area of outstanding natural beauty and designed with great taste and expertise. They have been able to explore a range of facilities and amenities aimed at all tastes and age groups. Because pre-planning has been thoroughly undertaken, they have been freed from the miseries of overcrowding and waiting as there is the optimum amount of space and equipment. They have been able to experiment under the guidance of expert staff who are friendly and relaxed but who keep a low profile. It is small wonder that such complexes attract tourists from many different European countries. Under these circumstances, it is highly likely that a large number of British visitors will discover some physical skill or develop some interest, thus creating a positive desire for happiness and fitness that will last throughout life. Some indeed, might even take up a sport and exploit a talent to a high level.

So what opportunities will these holiday-makers find when they get back home for pursuing newly-discovered sports and games in their leisure time? More than you might think. Britain is not favoured by the same even climate as the Mediterranean nor are amenities always concentrated so conveniently in idyllic coastal settings. Nevertheless, everything which they have experienced abroad is already available at home. For several years now, some of the best brains in this country have been occupied in meeting the demands set by returning travellers who have had a chance to experience their dreams of recreation.

New technology

New technology is speeding up the pace of the leisure revolution. In the past, the climatic and geographical features in any given area dictated the nature of leisure opportunities available. For example, a few favoured locations had a monopoly on natural advantages for those who wished to climb, ski or sail. Areas inhabited by the greatest concentration of people offered little in the way of excite- ment or novelty, so that sport and physical activity were too often confined to participation in traditional team games or in passive spectating. This is no longer the case. Cheap and easy travel has become available to so many of us now that with sufficient interest and determination, we can experiment with almost any activity which captures our imagination. If a site offers something particu- larly attractive, customers with time and money will seek it out and patronize it, which is an undeniable formula for success and satisfaction all round.

Because our climate is not always kind to sportspersons, artificial provisions are always going to cater for the great bulk of the population. Multi-purpose indoor sports halls for instance, are always going to be more consistently in use than beaches. Thus the artificial element has recently expanded rapidly ... appallingly, some might say. Whether you consider 'synthetic' attractions to be a blessing or a curse is a matter of personal opinion, but the fact remains that they are a part of contemporary life.

Attitudes to leisure are changing constantly. Consider these quotations from a Penguin book called *Synthetic Fun*, by Jeremy Sandford and Roger Law, which was published in 1967.

> Say what is the social needs for synthetic fun? The answer comes: affluence – leisure – and, above all, boredom – terrifying, hitherto unprecedented, BOREDOM ... Boredom has thrown up like an ugly pustule its own malaise. And, witnessing the world of synthetic fun, we may be struck by the amazing absence in Britain of any real thinking about leisure, any real orientation of education towards leisure, any attempt at planning for it.

We are attempting to educate and plan for leisure now. We are devoting thought to the direction in which we are travelling as the indoor amusement stadium of the past is replaced by the theme park of today. Consider these offers, which are all taken from recent advertisements, as evidence of the changes that are taking place:

```
Surf the breakers through a tropical jungle in
our surfing pool. Swim in the tropical lagoon
with real waves. There's a jungle pool for
toddlers, with a friendly croc and Sammy Sea
Snake. Relax in a constant climate of 80
degrees, and get a golden tan on one of the
Centre's many sun beds. Number one fun —
whatever the weather.
```

Take the NEW PROKON SUPER X SIMULATOR and experience a space-age ride of your life; fly in a helicopter, ride the white-water rapids and discover a journey into the unknown.

It's fun . . . it's exciting . . . it's Dry Slope Skiing! All slopes are laid with white Dendrix Matting and are fully floodlit. Instruction is available at all levels of skiing. Equipment is provided within the hourly rate.

The 'Subtropical Swimming Paradise' at Center Parcs Elvedon Forest Village. The temperature is maintained at 84°F all the year round, and exotic plants give the illusion of being far away from Britain.
(Photograph courtesy of Center Parcs Ltd.)

Golf Driving Range. Take your pick from 24 individual undercover floodlit bays, and practise your drive in all weathers. Aim for the target flags or splash pools for precise target golf. With a basket of 50 or 100 balls, you can spend your time sharpening up your game in preparation for the course without having to pick up a single golf ball.

On the deep mine tour visitors descend by special vehicle down Britain's steepest passenger incline railway. They alight at the bottom to follow, on foot, the life of a Victorian miner, in sound and light, through ever more dramatic chambers, including one containing a magnificent underground lake.

However, the fact that some of the experiences offered are rather obvious imitations of reality does worry some observers. Yet such attractions have proved to be popular with leisure seekers. Perhaps, after all, wave-simulators and plastic turf are an advance on rectangular Victorian swimming baths and recreation grounds surfaced with cinders. The point is that ingenuity and technical advances mean that we can now take the sites to the people as well as the people to the sites.

Trends in the leisure industry

Accurate predictions are hard to make, but it does appear there will be more, rather than less, emphasis on physical activity in leisure time. There is a conviction that leisure which is occupied with idleness or passive viewing of popular sports is dangerously unhealthy. The Scottish Health Council neatly gets this message across with its slogan: 'Cars and chairs cause body rust'. The media have revived interest in, and promoted knowledge about, exercise, and we have learned that we will live longer if we are not overweight and have some knowledge of healthy eating and drinking habits. Most of us know from personal experience that fitness generates a feeling of physical and mental well-being. So at the present moment fitness is in fashion.

Another trend has been the shift from team games towards individual activities where competition is less important. Conse-

If children discover that exercise can be fun the fitness habit will remain with them throughout their lives. (Photograph courtesy of John Walmsley.)

quently, there has been a rise in demand for keep-fit classes, modern dance sessions, gyms, squash courts and badminton courts. For the same reason, 'new' sports, such as orienteering have become popular.

The discovery that exercise can be fun and the desire to make more of life in every way are a reflection of a better system of education. Not everyone wishes to become a top athlete, but many are looking for ways of correcting lack of fitness caused by a sedentary way of life and to develop physical confidence. In addition, the young and the not so young are discovering that swimming and slimming clubs, just as much as discos and dances, are good ways of meeting people. The fact that such groups also communicate added knowledge about nutrition and healthy living is a welcome bonus. The leisure movement is then, helping to bring about the aim of a healthy and contented society. Both central and local government are realising that it is prudent to spend money in furthering this positive aim, in the hope of spending less on medical care and the provision of delinquency programmes.

Any organisation which funds projects will be anxious to see that the money it provides is spent effectively. In addition to being generally philanthropic or, at least well-intentioned, those who provide leisure facilities (especially in the private sector) are becoming increasingly concerned with efficient management and profitability.

This means that choosing the right type of person to be employed in the leisure industry has become an issue of paramount import-ance. The word 'industry' does seem like a contradiction in terms, because we are used to thinking of leisure as relaxing and amusing, and industry as being associated with grinding, mechanical work. The fact is though, that leisure has become big business, with a multi-million pound turnover and enormous capital investment. The leisure industry provides jobs for hundreds of thousands of men and women, and brings economic prosperity to areas which would otherwise have become very impoverished once the demand for their traditional products and skills had declined. One person's enjoy-ment is another person's employment.

Organisation, guidance and supervision are necessary for almost any activity. Facilities, equipment, accommodation and clothing are often essential. As a result, there are now many employment opportunities and rewarding professional careers for candidates with the right qualifications, skills and temperament.

The needs and capabilities of the individual customer are at the heart of the leisure industry, for we all have different aspirations: just as some of us dream of playing on the Centre Court at Wimbledon or scoring a century at Lords, others will see themselves as potential actors or musicians.

Leisure time need not be spent in sport or the performing arts. There are people who find their pleasure in travel or study. Some seek to find a role in society by caring for others, as is evidenced by the continuing popularity of the St. John's Ambulance Brigade, the Red Cross, the Women's Voluntary Service and similar organisations.

Whether one chooses, however, to devote one's free time to ice-dancing, boxing, mountaineering, choral singing, pool or yoga, the most important factor is the quality of the teacher, guide or organiser who transfers his or her enthusiasm and knowledge.

This applies whether the leisure pursuits are physical or mental, aggressive or contemplative, sociable or individual, high-risk or gently relaxing.

In the next chapter we shall look at the gradual increase in the amount of leisure time available to the working population, and the way in which provision for recreation has evolved since the Industrial Revolution ... from municipal park to Center Parc, you might say! The following table illustrates the wide range of sports and games that are available.

Table I   Some popular indoor and outdoor sports

Indoor (ground based)
Squash, badminton, indoor tennis, table-tennis,
netball, handball, volley-ball, basketball, indoor soccer,
weight training, weight lifting, gymnastics,
boxing, wrestling, judo, karate, fencing,
trampolining, ten-pin bowling, indoor bowling, skating (ice and roller),
small-bore shooting, billiards, snooker, pool, yoga.

Indoor (water based)
Swimming, water polo, formation swimming, octopush, life-saving.

Outdoor (ground based)
Soccer, rugby, cricket, hockey,
croquet, rounders, tennis, lacrosse,
athletics, cycling, shooting,
riding, mountaineering, rambling, orienteering,
golf, bowls, speed skating,
auto-cross, moto-cross, go-karting, rallying,
skiing, parachuting, gliding.

Outdoor (water based)
Swimming, scuba-diving, water-skiing, para-sailing,
sailing, rowing, canoeing, boating.

---

2   How did it begin?

If we study the history of our industrial society, we will learn that leisure and fresh air, freedom and fitness were, for most of the population, hard-won privileges. The denial of leisure time to industrial workers, and the attitude of most nineteenth-century employers who regarded them simply as 'hands', meant that millions of men, women and children lived short, unhappy lives.

The Industrial Revolution

In a hundred years, Britain changed from being a mainly agricultural country to a mainly industrial one. In about 1760 there occured the initial stage of a sequence later known as the Industrial Revolution. The increase in, and redistribution of, the population during this period was remarkably rapid and totally unplanned. It led to tremendous social and cultural problems and altered attitudes to work and recreation which had remained fixed for centuries.

In 1760, eight out of every 10 British people lived in the country-side, yet by 1860, only five out of every 10 lived in the country. The process continued into the twentieth century so that by 1950 only two out of 10 lived in the country. At the present time, it is estimated that the number of country-dwellers has shrunk to the almost incredible figure of five in every 100.

The figures of British population growth speak for themselves. From 1760 to 1830, the figure increased from about eight million to 16 million. By 1851, it was nearer 21 million. The crucial difference was that while 13 million of these still lived in small towns and villages, eight million had become crowded together in large towns where the new textile and engineering industries had developed, where raw materials were extracted or processed and where great ports had grown up. A few examples will make this clear.

From 1801 to 1851 the populations of Leeds and Birmingham went up by over 200 per cent. Liverpool, Manchester and Glasgow grew by more than 300 per cent. Most startling of all, the number of inhabitants in Bradford soared by no less than 700 per cent! Even

The backyard of a London slum. This picture was taken about 1930 and shows that in some towns and cities there was little space for exercise and play.
(Photograph by Edith Tudor Hart from *The World's Best Photographs*. Odhams Press, London.)

the older, more established cities, such as Norwich, Bristol and Edinburgh, doubled their size during this period.

Sprawling, unplanned growth led to horrifying slums, and these, in turn, produced chronic ill-health in the work-force. It must be borne in mind that rural life had never been idyllic for the labouring poor but, at least, there was no overcrowding or the transmission of diseases that inevitably followed it. Up to the eighteenth century, the pattern of life in the British countryside was determined by the seasons, which gave natural periods of inactivity. There were still vestiges of the medieval tradition of religious festivals when the observance of holy days (which gave us our word 'holiday') meant that all work was supposed to stop. At one time, there were as many as a 100 days a year which were designated holy days. Such days, however, were often an enforced rest from employment, and the concept of 'holy-day pay' was quite unknown!

The origins of most of the key aspects of our modern concept of leisure can be seen in earlier religious celebrations and observances. For example, the eating and drinking which accompanied occasions such as Christmas, harvest festivals and so on, are related to our present-day hospitality, just as traditional games, sports and dancing had an element of what we would now call physical recreation. Our idea of arts and entertainment would be fulfilled by miracle and mystery plays, while the connection with trade and commerce came whenever a fair was held!

Quality of life

The arrival of industrial, urban-based work was a physical and cultural shock to families trying to earn a living in the early days of the Industrial Revolution. It may be argued that industrialisation simply made worse long-existing evils, and concentrated levels of filth and infection. This was especially so because housing was usually inadequate. In Liverpool, for example, out of a population of 200,000, 56,000 lived in crowded courtyard tenements, while 20,000 actually lived in cellars with earth floors and no windows.

The great machines of the major manufacturing industries along with their gigantic steam engines had to be housed in towering factories, around which were clustered the houses of the workforce. The result of this was that noise and suffocating smoke surrounded the operatives in their homes, just as they did during their working day. Because wages tended to be very low, whole families, including the very young and the old, had to work long hours in order to survive.

There was no question of taking a stroll after work in the fresh air, not only because most people were too tired, and spent any spare time recuperating in readiness for the next day's efforts, but also because pleasant places to walk were hard to find in the vicinity of industrial towns and cities. The following passage from *The Illustrated London News* of 1861 sums up the situation in a few words:

Forty years ago good salmon were taken in the Thames. The walks along the Thames were pleasant places in those days. How changed now is the River and its banks! The former has become a filthy sewer; the fish have been destroyed.

The connection between the environment and disease did not go unnoticed. Edwin Chadwick was a tireless propagandist who advocated the need for public health regulations in the new industrial conurbations. In his *Report on the Sanitary Condition of the Labouring Poor*, which was published in 1842, he gave some startling statistics. For instance, he stated that in a rural area the average life expectancy for a gentleman was 52 years, and for a working man it was 38 years. The picture was horrifyingly different in the industrial towns. For example, life expectancy for a gentleman in Leeds was 44 years, and for a working man it was 19 years. Liverpool comes bottom of the list in this respect. There, a gentleman could expect to live to the age of 35 years, but the average age of death for a working 'man' was just 15 years! These are average figures, and they are made low by the high incidence of child mortality. According to Dr Andrew Combe's estimates, made in 1840, the percentage of infants who died in London before the age of five years during the period 1790–1809 was 41.5 per cent. The *Dictionary of Statistics (1899)* shows that even as late as 1880, 23.8 per cent of infants in England and Wales died before the age of five years.

The low level of life expectancy was also due to epidemics of such infectious diseases as diphtheria and cholera. Disease swept like wildfire through the unhygienic, over-populated urban areas. This dreadful situation led to activity on the part of social reformers and philanthropists, which eventually resulted in the passing of public health Acts and factory Acts. As the nineteenth century progressed, these Acts gradually remedied the appalling situations brought about by the Industrial Revolution.

Statistics and reports can sometimes make dull reading, but when we realise that they are summaries of decades of human misery, they begin to acquire importance to those of us who are studying what leisure can do to improve the quality and span of life.

Consider how a little leisure would have enriched the lives of the children mentioned in the *Second Report of the Children's Employment Commission (1843)*:

If the statements be correct, one of her children, four years of age, works 12 hours a day with only an interval of a quarter of an hour for each meal at breakfast, dinner and tea and never going out to play: and two more of her children, one six and the other eight years of age, work in summer from 6 am till dusk, and in winter from 7 in the morning till 10 at night; 15 hours.

Acts of Parliament

It was as a result of revelations such as these that Parliament reluctantly introduced a whole series of factory Acts, which during the period 1833–1937 did much to improve the lot of factory workers and miners. The principal results of these measures were to give safer working conditions and also to give more leisure time for adults and more opportunity for the education of children. Education brought benefits to all citizens as the nineteenth century progressed. The extract below appeared in the *Cornhill Magazine* in 1861:

> The school buildings in general are large and commodious, well-warmed and ventilated. Convenient playgrounds are in many cases attached to them and fitted up with swings, vaulting-poles and other games apparatus. Others have gardens cultivated by the boys, or workshops where a little carpentering is done.

These provisions seem surprisingly modern and are similar to the activities found in schools today where hobbies, school orchestras, drama, art appreciation, camping holidays and trips abroad are widely accepted as important components of education. This is particularly important in an age when fewer individuals are engaged in manual occupations, which are demanding in terms of time and physical energy. Formerly, relaxation was the prime aim of leisure, whereas with less emphasis on physical work, physical activities are increasingly in demand.

Later Acts of Parliament increased the powers of local authorities. However, many authorities were badly organized and could not or, sadly, would not take adequate steps to remedy the abuses that had sprung from advances in industrial technology.

Through the pressure exerted by the educated and enlightened sectors of society, local authorities began to realize that a positive attitude to public health was the best way to combat ill-health and the incidence of diseases. Some of the more forward-looking towns had, as early as the mid-nineteenth century, provided public baths and wash houses for the poor. Some even provided recreational and social amenities such as public parks, bowling greens, tennis courts, art galleries, museums, libraries, playing fields, and swimming baths (as opposed to just 'baths', which were for cleanliness and not exercise). This was the dawn of the era when local authorities became the prime provider of leisure facilities. In Manchester and Salford, for instance, in 1846, three public parks were opened 'To enable working-class people to enjoy games and recreation in the fresh air.'

It was a public health act which gave the greatest impetus to attempts to give encouragement to leisure activities. Part IV of the

Halifax Civic Park, 1864. There is a long tradition of 'pleasure grounds' for the relaxation of the urban masses having been provided by town and borough councils.

1875 Act laid down, among other things, regulations with regard to public pleasure grounds. This was an acknowledgment at least, that amenities and recreational facilities were connected with public health – if only indirectly.

As always, some authorities were more enthusiastic than others in fulfilling their obligations in a positive way. Birmingham Town Council spoke of: 'Sweeping away streets in which it was not possible to live a healthy and decent life: making the town cleaner, sweeter, brighter: providing gardens, parks and a museum.' Other municipal authorities took pride in showing concern for their citizens; after all, great wealth had been generated by successful industrial centres, and they proudly displayed it in the form of palatial town halls, magnificent civic centres and (by the standards of the time) generous provision of civic amenities for their less fortunate fellows. The movement to make leisure facilities available to all caught on, and to the grants from Parliament and town halls were added large sums raised by public subscription, as well as generous gifts from local philanthropists.

Spare time – a luxury

Unfortunately, the spread of all these worthwhile efforts was not as rapid as the expansion of industry had been. A great part of the problem was simply the lack of time free from work obligations. Free time was the greatest luxury of all.

It seems sadly ironic that factory work during the Industrial Revolution was extremely labour intensive, and in the first few decades of the nineteenth century the labouring poor worked longer hours and had fewer holidays than in medieval times. Nevertheless, the situation did improve slightly – before the mid-century, disposable income per head of the population began to rise as working hours become shorter. The working week, which had been about 84 hours over seven days in 1800, came down to about 70 hours over six days by 1870. This may seem a very long working week compared with the 35 to 38 hour week spread over five days that we have today, but in the last century a 60 or 70 hour week did offer the prospect of some spare time.

Many of the working population also benefited from the Bank Holiday Act of 1871. This measure, which slipped quietly through Parliament without much opposition because of its name, gave workers a legal right to fixed holidays at Christmas, Easter, and Whitsun, and an additional break in August.

Unfortunately, leisure time was not always used positively. Much work of the period was a grinding routine of daily drudgery often carried out in unpleasant physical conditions, so it is little wonder that, in their free time, both men and women sought refuge in drink. The violence, lawlessness and damage done to family relationships as a result of intemperance was so great, that 'the demon, drink' was regarded as a threat to the social fabric. Factors such as these led some people to give leisure a bad name.

Attitudes to leisure

The monied classes had a very biased attitude to leisure. Sport (in the form of field sports), culture and recreation were considered the privilege of the wealthy: the poor were expected to make do with devotion to God, thrift and contentment with their lot. Many of the employers of the period belonged to the new, prosperous middle class, and were zealously religious-minded. They had read in both the Old Testament and the New Testament that work was God's original intention for man. They saw divine wisdom in the verse from the book of Genesis in which man was told quite clearly: 'You shall gain your bread by the sweat of your brow.' Work became regarded as the path to self-respect and salvation, to sobriety and prosperity.

The problem then arose that employers had to allow some time off work on Sundays, because as non-conformist preachers reminded them, the book of Exodus had commanded: 'Six days shall you labour and do all your work.' The church, ever mindful of the thought that 'the Devil finds work for idle hands to do', laid down a full schedule of attendance at religious services and Sunday school classes. The idea that leisure activities could occupy idle hands occurred only to the most progressive thinkers of the time.

The true purpose of leisure, its essential, valuable content, should be: relaxation, personal development and community participation. Yet, because the puritanical ethos current during the Industrial Revolution has dominated the British attitude to leisure for generations, we have never had the free-and-easy appreciation of unoccupied time that exists in Mediterranean countries or the USA. In America, for instance, leisure time is regarded as a right and as an essential amenity. In Britain, free time often produced a feeling of guilt or inadequacy. Nineteenth-century teaching gave rise to such economic, religious and social pressures that whole-hearted enjoyment and relaxation were frowned upon. To be fair, the attitudes of the authorities and the church were, to some extent, understandable. Drunkenness and barbaric sports, such as cock-fighting, dog-fighting and bull-baiting, were not by any civilized standards a valid use of leisure time, so there was a backlash against 'idleness and vice', and the view arose that only productive work was a worthwhile use of time. Work came first, and about the only excuse for playing games was the desire to ensure a healthy mind in a healthy body. The social climate changed as the century progressed, but even in our own day the modern concept that we should have as much leisure as possible for as many people as possible has many opponents, and is not yet totally respectable!

The impact of cheap travel

Other factors were at work though, to make the lives of our Victorian ancestors a little more pleasurable and profitable. That 'unholy marriage of coal and iron' that had given birth to the Industrial Revolution, had also created steam transport and a railway system that expanded rapidly. By 1846, 272 Acts of Parliament had been passed authorising new railway routes, and there were over 3,000 miles of track, 'railway mania' was at its height.

Because of the comparative cheapness of third-class rail fares, more and more working class people were able to make trips away from home. The rail network continued to grow, so that by 1883 there were 16,200 miles of track, and almost 20,000 by 1903. Railways widened horizons in a way which must have been more dramatic than we can now imagine. Some commentators were quick to see the beneficial possibilities of this new form of travel, as is shown by this extract from *Chamber's Journal* which was published on 21 September 1844:

> Not the least important effect is the facilities they [the railways] have afforded the humbler classes for recreation. Short trips give the working classes the opportunity of that which they would never have been able, under the old stage coach and wagon dynasty, to behold. The artisan, cooped up and constantly breathing bad air, has now the opportunity, on every available holiday, of making excursions to the country ... nothing opens men's minds so much as seeing a variety of things, of places and of men.

Holidays could be spent further away from home, theatre companies toured the country, sports teams travelled further afield, the exchange of information and views was greatly speeded up and facilitated.

In 1841, Thomas Cook organised his first excursion by railway when 570 passengers were carried at one shilling per head on a special train. With astonishing energy, Cook used the 'permanent way' to transport people for their entertainment – first, in the 1840s, to Scotland and, by 1872, right round the world.

Later in the century, the invention of the pedal-driven bicycle brought a great increase in trips to the countryside and the seaside by individuals and cycle touring clubs. Although early motor cars appeared on the roads of Europe in the 1880s, they were at that time merely expensive toys for the very rich. Nevertheless, the development of the internal combustion engine was surprisingly rapid, and by the turn of the century motor charabancs were plying a healthy trade between the towns, with trips to the coast and to the country for sightseeing and pleasure.

The rise of the seaside resort

The most exciting result of shorter hours and cheap travel was the opening up of the British seaside. The restorative possibilities of the coast had been appreciated by the rich in much earlier times, when fashionable society flocked in carriages to the seaside in search of the magic healing properties of mineral waters, sea bathing, fresh air and sunshine. Brighton, Margate and Scarborough were all originally spas or 'watering places'. whose popularity boomed in the mid-nineteenth century, as railways brought the coast within reasonable reach of the masses.

Entertainments soon grew up to amuse this influx of newcomers: the 'diversions', as they were called, included fairgrounds and floral halls, music halls, 'winter gardens' (for music and dancing), Punch and Judy shows, peepshows, and piers, which evolved from simple landing jetties into fun complexes. Resorts in North Wales got rather more than their fair share of piers. It was soon discovered that quaint fishing villages in Wales were within easy reach by sea from Liverpool. The paddle-boat, powered by the universal miracle of steam, transported hundreds of thousands of workers for a short respite from the teeming slums of Merseyside to the ozone-rich shores and headlands of such places as Rhyl, Colwyn Bay and Llandudno.

Street entertainers migrated from the towns and cities for the summer season, and established themselves in tented booths on the beaches. Musicians and minstrels, players and showmen of all kinds, discovered to their joy that people on holiday spend more freely than at home. Some players established seaside theatres and marine halls, others performed at the end of the pier in the elaborately decorated pavilions. Seaside borough councils emerged as enthusiastic suppliers of attractions, and, as they prospered, the resorts vied with one another to build promenades, parks and gardens, big wheels, tramways, cable railways and landmark monuments such as the famous Blackpool Tower. There must have been a heady atmosphere at the seaside in those early days, as pale workers from the factories in the towns revelled in the fresh air and their temporary escape from the daily routine. From the literature of the period, we can see that there was a spirit of freedom from restraint. The bustling resorts with miles of golden sands and garish amusements must have seemed as romantic and exotic in the last century as Mediterranean holiday venues first seemed to a later generation in an era of package tours and cheap air travel.

Not all holiday-makers and trippers of the period went in search of gaudiness and noise. For some travellers, their reason for visiting the coast was (and still is) to find quiet coves and rocky headlands where they might admire the view. Those seeking rest and relaxation would seek out quiet harbours and picturesque ports, rolling downland and the remote green lanes of the countryside. Whether the new class of leisure seekers demanded 'lively' resorts or 'unspoiled' ones, accommodation had to be provided for their seasonal stays. Rows upon rows of seaside boarding houses were hastily erected from about 1830 onwards, which offered modest bed and board at reasonable prices, and there was a vogue for weekend cottages in beauty spots. For more affluent visitors, splendid.

purpose-built hotels were constructed at vantage points overlooking the sea. The seaside visit had become an institution – a constant feature of the British way of life.

Every institution which has a well-marked and charted rise, has, sooner or later, a corresponding decline, the novelty wears off and consumers seek new sensations. So it seemed to be with the British seaside holiday. In the two decades following the Second World War holiday-makers began to look abroad, and aided by another travel revolution, this time an airborne one, were beginning to seek sunnier beaches and fresh, foreign sensations. British resorts made noble efforts to compete with cheap holidays abroad, but they could not alter the British weather. The organisers of holiday entertainment in Britain did their best to adapt to changing leisure patterns and, indeed, they have proved expert at continuously updating the facilities they offer. Now the wheel seems to be coming full circle, for a survey conducted in 1991 indicates that British-based holidays are preferred by 82 per cent of potential customers. Such decisions may have been influenced by factors such as congested airports, resorts ruined by over-urbanisation, and the soaring cost of foreign travel, which is all too often accompanied by declining standards of hospitality. But principally it is a phenomenon known as 'sub-tropical Britain' which is encouraging Britons to holiday at home. Three-quarters of those questioned in the survey said that bad weather would not put them off if they could have indoor pool complexes, luxury accommodation and good sporting facilities. In the last five years, there has been a great increase of such provision, and most major seaside resorts have, or are planning, their sun centres, holiday worlds, entertainment worlds, theme parks, sub-tropical swimming paradises, and so on. The essential feature of these centres is a sort of space-age greenhouse, a futuristic glass dome offering a wide range of indoor and outdoor sports and a choice of continental bars, bistros and restaurants. The point is that you can swim or laze beneath palm trees and exotic plants at sub-tropical 84°F – even in the frozen depths of winter. Self-catering is becoming the order of the day, with a massive 98 per cent saying that freedom to do what they want, and being able to eat when and where they please as a family will make them choose self-catering. Such innovations as those outlined above would mean that holiday breaks could be staggered so that seaside and country resorts would not have to rely as heavily on a brief summer season and corresponding seasonal employment.

Present-day holiday-makers seem to be more sophisticated and discriminating than their forebears. As a result, seaside sport is now much more ambitious and varied, but in addition it appears there is a growing thirst for information and education. There are few tourist towns that omit to give details of interesting features, such

Nowadays, canal boat holidays are a very popular alternative to the traditional seaside break.

(Courtesy of the British Waterways Board.)

as wildlife sanctuaries, nature trails, stately homes and castles, country parks and the sites of industrial archaeology, that are within easy reach. It is perhaps strange that in a new era of leisure we visit, as alternative attractions to the beaches, the mills, tin mines, slate mines and forges where our ancestors slaved to earn a living and, possibly, a little precious leisure time!

The evolution of modern society

All this is a far cry from the hard times and chaotic conditions of the early days of the Industrial Revolution. To discover how modern society gradually evolved, we must glance back again at the troubled history of industrialisation. The pace of progress is often dictated by the thoughts and actions of great men and women, and there were some reformers whose humanitarian views gradually gained acceptance in the nineteenth century. Lord Shaftesbury, known as 'the children's friend', was the person who, perhaps more than anyone else, forced members of Parliament to do something about conditions in the factories. Shaftesbury, a rich, well-educated, and deeply religious man, was shocked when he discovered the conditions in which the poor lived and worked. His decision to do something practical led to the Factory Act of 1833, and a succession of other Acts, which slowly but surely improved the lot of the people. Richard Oastler, a Yorkshire business-man, and Michael Sadler, a Yorkshire MP, worked for years and sacrificed their own time and money to get Parliament to pass more Acts to help the workers.

The greatest practical example that paved the way for our modern view that workers and citizens are not expendable, but valuable assets, was given by Robert Owen's factory at New Lanark. When he took the factory over in 1800 it had 2,000 workers. Of these, 400 were children, some as young as five years old. There were all the usual evils of the period – slum dwellings, crime and drunkenness, long working hours, sickness and premature death. He set out to change all this. He abolished child labour and set up schools for children and their parents. He shortened hours of work so that people had time and opportunity for leisure. He built good homes for his employees, with gardens where they could grow their own food, as well as shops where essentials could be bought at reasonable prices. The result was that his workers were contented; they worked hard and the factory prospered.

There was no instant reaction by other industrialists to the lesson taught by Owen's experience, but over the years the wisdom of his system was seen by some thoughtful and humanitarian employers, and by the end of the century a few pioneers were facing up to the social problems created by bad housing and bad health. The idea of a model industrial community was taken up by Lord Leverhulme, who in 1888 built for his workers the spacious and pleasant village of Port Sunlight near Liverpool. His example was followed in 1895 by Mr Cadbury, who planned the green and leafy suburban town of Bournville. The concept was carried into the twentieth century when, as a result of the 'garden city' movement, Letchworth was founded in 1903, Hampstead Garden Suburb in 1907, and Welwyn Garden City in 1920. The garden city movement insisted that green spaces promoted positive health and made possible the enjoyment of leisure time.

Public health statistics also showed that, at the lowest level of advantage, improved housing produced a fitter, happier workforce which, in turn, led to efficiency, productivity and social responsibility. Both public and Parliamentary opinion had been shocked by the *Report of the Select Committee on Physical Deterioration*, which commented on the large proportion of recruits for the Boer War (1899–1902), who possessed sub-standard physiques and suffered from poor health and fitness.

After the First World War (1914–18), it had become usual for civic housing authorities to provide good-sized gardens and allotments where horticultural pursuits were carried out and fresh vegetables could be grown, for they had taken to heart the obvious truth that the homes and gardens of a country show more clearly than anything else, the way in which a people live.

The lack of space in the decaying inner cities which were the legacy of the Industrial Revolution, taken with the statistics of an ever-growing population, led planners to develop the idea of 'new towns' after the Second World War. In the 1950s, Harlow and Crawley were built to absorb the overspill from the London area, and the process was continued with the construction of a second generation of new towns such as Milton Keynes, Telford, Washington (Tyne and Wear), and others, some of which are still being built. The planners of these towns realised that most people have a need for leisure and educational opportunities inside and outside the home and tried to ensure suitable spaces and amenities.

Looking back over the last 150 years, we have to conclude that the growth in population and the rise of a machine civilisation have led to advances in social welfare; and during the last 50 years we have come to take for granted comforts and amusements that had not previously been dreamed of. The age of iron and steam left a dreadful legacy of blackened factories, slag heaps, factory chimneys, rusting railway lines and untidy canals, while the unplanned concentration of population into ugly rows and tenement barracks left hundreds of acres of crumbling brickwork which were unfit for human habitation. We are now spending much time and money on salvaging and preserving some of these industrial areas, and package tours to 'historic Bradford' and Liverpool's Albert Dock, for instance, are attracting hordes of tourists. Despite the problems, the inhabitants of machine-age cities gradually won a degree of leisure and a predictable pattern of free hours which had been unknown in the days of peasant agriculture and cottage industry. People began to eat better and to live longer. Team games, especially soccer, began to be played, and attracted huge crowds of spectators. Between 1863 and 1886, national associations were founded in Britain for soccer, rugby, cycling, boxing, hockey and tennis. There was also an upsurge in clubs, institutes, newspapers, music halls, choirs and participation in municipal democracy.

Such benefits were linked inextricably with urban industrialism and began to form a basis for civilised living as the workforce, particulary the skilled machine operatives, became more prosperous. Increasing riches went to the ordinary man, and real wages in Britain between 1850 and 1900 rose by 50 per cent. Two hundred years before this period, people had lived and died in the place where they were born, and had no independent life outside their family and the local community. In cities, unattractive though the environment was, they were able to seek more personal fulfilment and social development.

After the First World War, electric trams and trains and the

Motor caravans were popular in the late 1920s.

coming of 'motoring for the masses' made possible the building of residential suburbs at a distance from the factories. We can now see with the advantage of hindsight that haphazard building sprawl is itself a bad thing, but at least the new 'green field' sites did provide a healthier and more pleasant way of life at the time. The revolution in personal transport which began in the first half of this century has created a whole range of activities which go far beyond the need to travel from A to B. Just as in the nineteenth century the invention of the bicycle led to the formation of cycle touring clubs and cycle racing, the spread of car ownership gave rise to new interests such as caravan touring, motor rallying and motor racing. Motoring for pleasure has, in fact, led to a huge spectrum of provision and facilities in locations away from urban centres.

Modern trends

Nowadays, leisure in all its aspects has become not just respectable, but a valued part of the national economy. Leisure provision, which began as a beneficient social service, has, with the advent of competition from private sources, become much more customer orientated and imaginative. Potential users of leisure facilities are now wooed by promises of 'A break taken when you need it rather than when custom dictates', and the understanding comment that: 'With everyday life ever more frenetic, there's an overwhelming need to unwind'. The emphasis now seems to be that leisure and the enjoyment of it is something which we deserve, and we are told 'You owe it to yourself to get away from all the tensions of the working life' . . . and all this in spite of the fact that the whole concept of the relationship between work and leisure has also changed beyond all recognition! Work in our day has, generally, become more pleasurable or, at least, more tolerable than it was for our ancestors. It is likely to change even more dramatically as the electronic age gathers pace, and more sophisticated techniques of cybernetics and information technology shorten the working week and the working lifetime, as incidentally, they add to the possibility of newer ways to spend that additional free time.

Looking to the future, certain other trends are also apparent. The divisions between the traditional roles of the sexes are already becoming blurred, and this will continue so that more married women, who in our grandparent's generation took advantage of labour-saving devices to reduce domestic drudgery, will be enabled to take a job outside the home and still have more free time and more money to spend in it.

The well-established custom where working men retired at the age of 65, and working women at the age of 60, is also being questioned. On average we now live 12 years longer than we did 50 years ago, and we are much healthier than we were then because advances in medicine have eliminated many scourges of the past. The increasing number of deaths due to heart failure points, we are told, quite clearly to the conclusion that we need to take more exercise in our extra leisure time.

Demands for leisure provision and improved facilities are also being heard now from groups whose interests and problems have not hitherto been positively considered. Such bodies of consumers are often referred to as 'minority' groups, or 'special needs' groups. Classification of this type is artificial and, perhaps, rather slighting. We all have special needs and particular interests, and to categorise people by age, class, ethnic origin or physical capability does appear rather inappropriate in an industry which has as its first considera-tion the needs of the individual. Of course, as providers of facilities for leisure and recreation, we shall have to ensure at the planning stage that every potential user will be able to take advantage of what we have to offer, and may have to use 'labels' in our discussions. We shall consider these and other issues in the next chapter.

3 Who are the customers, and what do they want?

The leisure industry is, in the broadest sense, a caring industry, so it is essential for us to try to understand our customers, to discover where they work, how much free time they have, what skills and interests they have and, above all, we must maintain a dialogue with them to find out what they want of us since the rapid changes in social and economic conditions could lead to the provision of the wrong thing to the wrong people at the wrong time and place!

We live in the post-industrial age which has seen a decline in heavy industries, such as steel-making and ship-building, and in the extractive industries, such as mining and quarrying. One result of this is that manual skills have greatly diminished in importance, while technical skills have become increasingly vital in the fields of manufacturing and trade. Social class has traditionally determined both leisure time available and the type of leisure activity enjoyed. Nowadays, however, the old-fashioned distinction between 'blue-collar' (manual) and 'white-collar' (clerical) workers is becoming less clear cut as technology advances. There has been great change and expansion in the service occupations, such as hairdressing, nursing, catering, retail sales and transport, while new-style manufacturing concerns are demanding a fresh breed of clerical and administrative workers with skills in sophisticated systems of finance/stock control and information technology.

Changing work patterns

It is not just a different type of work, nor even the number of hours worked in the week, but the distribution of those hours which is changing the pattern of work obligation, so that we are no longer able to speak glibly of 'The normal work routine'. In many offices, there has been a greater adoption of 'flexitime', an arrangement by which an employee may vary his or her time of starting work, finishing work, taking a midday break or, in some cases, the number of days worked in a week. Flexitime had its origin in the need to spread the flow of road traffic pouring into city centres, but it could also have a marked effect on the leisure industry. The systems of split shifts that are now used by both manufacturing and service industries are much more complex than the old day-shift/night-shift pattern. The result of this is that members of a workforce often have time off early in the morning or late in the evening, sometimes for a week at a time, for a fortnight, for a month or even longer, so providers of leisure facilities must be aware of, and continuously adapt to, changes as they occur within their catchment area.

Automation, which was in its infancy during the first half of this century, has now moved far beyond the simple mechanisation of heavy work. Control and manipulation systems have advanced so that computers, electronic machines and industrial robots are able to perform extremely intricate tasks. As a result, it is estimated that jobs in the traditional manufacturing industries have declined by 30 per cent since 1960, and the average working week in this sector stands at 38 hours.

However, we should not simply assume that all working people have shorter hours. Working time for some members of the service industries mentioned above, and those engaged in the new industries, has actually increased so that their average working week now stands at an estimated 48 hours ... and that is only an average; some work considerably longer.

For rapidly expanding numbers of managers, data processors, designers, engineers and others subject to the influence of information technology, the working day has extended so that tasks and projects are simply not started at nine am and stopped at five pm. Portable telephones, lap-top computers, and fax machines mean that work can go on practically non-stop. A massive increase in global commerce and communication means that it is a working day for someone, somewhere ... all the time. As well as communication systems, faster travel has increased the volume and pace of business transactions so enormously that world commuting is almost as commonplace a work obligation as train and bus journeys were in the earlier years of this century. Little wonder, then, that in the information age the pressure of work is leading to a reduction of leisure and an increase of stress in both men and women. Not all those involved in a 'fast' lifestyle are hostile to it, because it is exciting and, if carried out efficiently, profitable – many individuals find it so engrossing that no distinction is made between work and leisure ... until they 'burn out', fall sick or ruin their family life.

One would imagine that leisure provision for such people should be relaxing and soothing. Paradoxically, though, they are often the ones who choose energetic, competitive and goal-directed activities.

What no one finds enjoyable is the unwelcome extension of work-related obligations caused by the crowded road, rail or air networks encountered when travelling to work. Such conditions which extend the working day and create dangerous stress, are likely to continue as long as living at a distance from one's place of work remains possible.

Such variations in the pattern of work should make us realise how precious leisure time is to customers, and how valuable local provision is in offering a service that will enhance the quality of life for clients who might be suffering from 'hurry sickness'.

Leisure for the retired

In the previous chapter we noted that the average person has, over the last 100 years, experienced a shorter working day and a shorter working week. We may also observe that almost everyone has a shorter working year, a shorter working life and a longer period of post-work life expectancy. This is largely due to improvements in medical facilities, better standards of living, conditions of work and the spread of health education, as well as a reduction in jobs involving heavy physical labour. All of this seems a positive gain until one considers that the overall result is that as methods of production change, some employees find themselves too near the end of their working lives to adapt or re-train, and are forced into accepting early retirement, which may initially create a gap in their social lives as many of their friendships and interests have always been work based.

At the same time that the elderly are enjoying greater vitality, they have also discovered that they have fewer duties, such as looking after grandchildren. Such duties ensured that their hobbies and pastimes were generally home based, if only because knitting, gardening, pigeon fancying, singing and story telling, for example, were compatible with childminding.

The traditional role of childminding has largely broken down as couples have fewer children, there is a trend towards one-parent families and there is greater social and geographical mobility. The result of all this is that we now have a generation of grandparents with more free time at their disposal.

Retired individuals who were thought of as old in the 1890s, are, in the 1990s, still enjoying a vigorous and healthy lifestyle. One wonders what a 'granny' of the last century would make of her present-day counterpart!

Retiring from work used to mean finishing with a regular income, but better state pensions and occupational pensions plus more foresight and planning, have removed the poverty which was a characteristic part of the lives of the old. In our time, a comfortable standard of living is more widespread for the retired and, given that national standards of affluence are maintained, there is likely to be a rising retirement leisure market. Evidence that this process is well under way is provided by a Department of Trade Study on Accidents at Home and During Leisure which was published in 1991:

> Among the sports becoming more popular with senior citizens are orienteering, gliding, caving, hang-gliding, windsurfing, mountaineering and underwater diving. Pensioners who take up risky sports have a better safety record than younger competitors. Elderly people are more likely to have the right training before tackling a potentially perilous sport.

Not all retired people, of course, are going to seek out such demanding sports, nor are they all going to have the means to indulge in them, but at least this is an indication that travel abroad, education and media coverage have raised the level of awareness and expectation of this growing sector of society. In any event, most providers of leisure have a variable pricing policy, which means that senior citizens are given substantial discounts. There is evidence from sports centres and the tourist industry that retired people are becoming regular customers, as they take up activities which they have only dreamed about during their working life. Some have

The range of leisure activities now available means that anyone can take up something they've never had a chance to do before. (Photograph courtesy of John Walmsley.)

always wanted to travel and are delighted to find that during the low season they can live more cheaply and comfortably by the Mediterranean than in their home town; others are able to pursue their studious and cultural interests by visiting museums, art galleries, theatres and stately homes, as well as attending festivals and courses. Flexible time stimulates flexible thinking, and stereotypes are fast disappearing.

The cost of leisure

Our own experience tells us that some leisure pursuits require more money than others, and no matter how much we may wish to follow some sport or interest, we find that the cost of equipment and/or club membership places them beyond our reach. Yet, present-day technology is so versatile that no ambition need be absolutely denied. Would-be skiers who cannot afford a season in St Moritz, can at least take note of the following advice from a leisure centre brochure:

> Using a dry ski slope can teach the basics to complete novices before their ski holiday, or give more advanced skiers the chance to get into shape before their annual holiday.
> We offer the chance to everyone to have a go at skiing without the initial expense of booking a winter sports holiday.
> Many people find artificial slope skiing an interesting and rewarding recreation in itself.

Working people's holiday allowances are often quite generous and a total of four weeks per year is common. Given that most people in work save with the sole aim of fulfilling a once-a-year ambition, even up-market pursuits such as yachting are within the reach of the masses, because a low-season, two-week sailing holiday around the Turkish coast can be had for as little as £230.

Generally speaking, the principal providers of opportunities for all-year-round sport and recreation in a given area will be the leisure and community services department of local councils, plus private clubs and centres. We shall look in more detail at the present generation of leisure centres in the next chapter, but a glance at local newspapers will reveal the enormous variety of facilities and attractions offered to the community by such centres. From humble beginnings in Victorian times, local authority services have become wide ranging and of a high standard. Competition with private facilities has often led to well-funded schemes which are welcoming and user friendly.

Using a dry ski slope can teach the basics to complete novices before their first ski holiday or give more experienced skiers the chance to get into shape.

(Photograph Dave Wallace.)

The paying public

To the question, 'Who are the customers?', we must answer that they are people whose needs and aims are as varied as their ages, jobs and capabilities. Not all of them will know exactly what they are looking for; as well as extrovert and confident sportspersons, there will be the shy, the diffident and the lonely. Different customers will have experienced different types of home life and some will be subject to unfamiliar social and religious customs which have to be treated with respect and understanding. Such factors have to be taken into consideration constantly, so that, properly organised and administered, the leisure centre can exert a tremendous cultural influence, which will work towards producing a fitter, happier, better-integrated society, just as the first generation of sports halls and games grounds did 100 years ago.

All who enter sports facilities must be given personal attention and made to feel at home. There will be no possibility of this if we do not realise that there are some potential customers who find access difficult.

Being disabled, unable to walk or drive a motor vehicle used to mean a life of being confined to home and dependent upon others. There are now so many types of wheelchairs, both powered and manually propelled, that people with mobility problems are able to take a greater part in the life of the community, and many public buildings, places of entertainment and centres of interest make a point of providing easy access for those with impaired mobility. Keeping active and exercising, especially in later life, can help people to stay mobile, so sports complexes and leisure centres should be in the forefront to improve access. We should make sure that we are well informed on such matters as diet and therapeutic exercise and information about aids which range from walking sticks and walking frames through wheelchairs and stairlifts to purpose-designed personal vehicles. A working knowledge of schemes and benefits, such as Mobility Allowance, would also be helpful.

Thinking on this subject is especially important where a centre plays host to a wide variety of sports clubs, and a positive effort should be made to attract clients. Perhaps the example of good practice, shown opposite, recently observed in the press will make this clear.

Strange to say, a group which has been greatly discriminated against in the past is the family. Everyone pays lip service to the importance of the family unit, but it has, until quite recently, been assumed that children and adults should be segregated in taking their recreation. Public houses even now have restrictions which prevent parents and their children under 14 sitting down to eat together. The attitude in clubs, hotels and leisure centres used to be

EVERYONE DESERVES A SPORTING CHANCE!

IRON WILLS – The Disabled Sports Club
Every Thursday night at the Sports Centre
6 pm–9 pm. . . . . Admission 50p.
Activities include: Table Tennis, Bowls,
Card and Board Games, Swimming,
Volleyball, Short Tennis, etc.
Games for the more severely handicapped
are available through the Club.
Transport can be arranged.
If you have able-bodied friends who would
like to help please ask them to come along.
(Admission free for helpers)
ALL WELCOME

that youngsters must have separate provision from adults. This is now changing. The director of a flourishing private sports club with a 15 month waiting list for membership, sums up the reasons for her success:

A large proportion of our membership are families, and this reflects our efforts to build up the club's social scene. There are no age restrictions, and unlike some clubs which do not liking admitting children under two to swimming sessions, we have parents bringing babies in at only four to five months old.

People do bring their children with them, and I think it's a case of educating them from an early age to be aware of fitness and sport. More and more parents are doing this, and engaging in activities as a family rather than as individuals.

Dot Downing, Director Shifnal Squash Club.

Local authority centres have also taken steps in this direction, as the following excerpt from a brochure illustrates:

Toddlers Gymnastics

Mums and dads, bring your under fives to the fun and tumble of toddlers' gymnastics, under the supervision of a qualified gym coach.

Parent and toddler

An opportunity for mother and baby (up to five years) to swim together under instruction for just 55p.

Family swim, 2 + 2 . . . . £2.40

Family swim (adult) 80p

Family swim (junior) 40p

Sometimes different members of the family have different interests, and wish to pursue separate activities in the same complex at the same time, so that to accompany a housewives' badminton session, a Saturday club (two hours of action-packed fun for seven to fourteen-year-olds, including soccer, rounders, cricket, badminton, athletics, tennis and assault courses) is thoughtfully arranged to cover the same period. There are also examples of sessions particularly aimed to occupy children at times when they might be bored, such as the following:

HOLIDAY SPORTS SCHEME

During the school holidays we hold an action-packed sports programme for all children to have fun and learn new sports including trampolining, cricket, five-a-side soccer, assault courses, canoeing, water polo and much more.

For special occasions there are always children's parties, for example an hour of activities followed by a tea party. One could give many more examples of family-orientated provision, for centre managers know that children will grow up into customers in their own right and catching potential customers young makes sound financial sense as well!

The needs of the customer

The above partly answer our other question. 'What do the customers want?' but there is much more, for as we have already noted, the boom in the use of leisure and sports facilities has created a demand for a steadily expanding range of activities. The customer wants everything that he or she can get, from sub-aqua swimming to the solarium and the sauna, and from aerobics to aikido. People want to shed pounds of ugly fat and achieve a healthy looking golden tan.

John Trower, the leisure services manager for a large area in Shropshire taking in both rural districts and high-density urban neighbourhoods, spoke from experience when talking about the customers' needs.

> Yes, more people are taking part in leisure. Health, fitness and general well-being of the individual are becoming very important, and that's had a spin-off at all our sports centres. I think it's true to say we have experienced growth in all our activities.
>
> The thing that we have to make sure, now that we are pulling them in, is that we keep them and make them feel that they have been properly looked after.

In the commercial sector where leisure facilities stand or fall by the numbers coming through the doors, such sentiments assume an even greater significance. Alan Durban the manager of a large racquet centre in Telford explained how demand had altered direction and how his organisation diversified to ensure continuing popularity:

> Whereas before people were only interested in profile and attracting large events here, and thinking they could survive on visitors, tennis tournaments, etc. we have spent more time making it a members' club, realising that we had to improve facilities and look after the members. This has led to investment in new outdoor tennis courts, a general revamp of the building, other improvements including an extension to the members' bar, new patios and a balcony overlooking the courts, and the purchase of new hydra fitness equipment.
>
> Our gymnastics and dance studios are more buoyant now than they have ever been, and I attribute the upsurge in health and fitness to more publicity on the subject.

So, fashions in the leisure field can be fickle, but customers will 'vote with their feet' and walk away to seek what they want elsewhere if their wants are not supplied. It is instructive to consider the following report of a council debate on keeping up with fitness fashions. The names of the district and the speakers have been omitted, but otherwise this is an exact transcription.

People in sedentary occupations are often the most eager to snatch any opportunity for exercise. The relatively simple equipment of the 'urban gyms' is rapidly being replaced by the hi-tech machines of fitness suites.

(Photograph courtesy of Powercise.)

CENTRE PROBING MOVES FOR A HEALTHIER INCOME

Moves to make the Sports and Leisure Centre users fitter – and its own income healthier – are being investigated.

Weight training and fitness equipment, such as treadmills, exercise bicycles and rowing-machines could be provided in a new fitness suite at the centre. This was the real growth area in leisure, and in a neighbouring centre a similar suite has more than 400 users a week, the manager said.

The equipment is popular not only for body-building, but for general aerobic work for people who want to improve their looks, rehabilitation, cardio-vascular improvement and strength, he told the Management Committee last night.

It was unlikely the centre would be able to buy the equipment and provide a new room to install it, but investigations had shown that leasing could be a viable alternative.

'It could be done by shutting a squash court and installing the fitness equipment there. But this centre, unusually, still has a full commitment to squash and it would be wrong to take away one of the courts when they are fully booked,' he added.

The Committee called for further investigations, which could also mean the existing small weight-training room being converted into a sauna. 'Even on conservative figures, this shows a potential profit of £25,000 a year.'

Several members expressed reservations about siting a portable building alongside the Centre to house the equipment.

While the Committee was investigating costs and siting possibilities, the manager of the other centre mentioned in the newspaper report had already installed his equipment and issued the following leaflet:

The Leisure and Community Services have branched out into

the world of Preventative Health Care.

Fitness Testing is available on an appointment basis.

Fitness assessment

In short the test comprises the following:
*screening   *blood pressure   *resting pulse
*weight   *body fat %   *lung capacity
*trunk flexibility   *aerobic capacity   *diet analysis

The stamina test is then conducted on a bicycle ergometer with heart rate monitored throughout. There are also tests of flexibility, followed by a discussion of the results and an exercise/diet prescription to suit your individual needs. The consultation cost is £10 per individual assessment £5 for a reassessment.

Use of Fitness Suite

£2.50 initial training session
£1.75 per hour after training and registration
£1.00 session Monday – Sunday 12.00 noon–2.00 pm

This illustration clearly shows that the public will make their wishes known, get what they want and pay for it. There has been a significant increase in participation in both indoor and outdoor sports, with nearly 50 per cent of all individuals over 15 taking part regularly in at least one activity. Just 8 per cent of us now habitually watch sport.

Fashions may be stimulated by media influences. Snooker and pool, for example, owe their sudden popularity to mass television coverage, and a recent (1991) *General Household Survey* reveals that in the period from 1987, 27 per cent of males in the UK took part in cue sports. Of those, 62 per cent were aged between 16 and 19. Swimming and diving were the favourite sports for women, with 13 per cent taking part, while 12 per cent of women went in for keep fit, yoga, aerobics and dance exercise. Surprisingly, the most popular form of sport is the oldest and simplest – walking, and 38 per cent of people interviewed listed it as their favourite recreation.

Men were found to have more free time than women (43 per cent had 10 hours or more at weekends, compared to 27 per cent of women). It is not then surprising that 63 per cent of men regularly participated in sport or exercise, as against 50 per cent of women.

There are other reasons for the increased popularity of physical activity, and Mary Fitzhenry of the Sports Council thinks it is because: 'Without doubt there has been a huge increase in the professionalism of leisure centre managers.' There is much truth in this, and certainly the successful managers are those who have come to terms with the new technology and tastes involved in leisure, and have made an effort to be innovative. This sort of attitude will become even more important after 1992 when a government bill to open up the management of municipal sports and leisure facilities to the private sector comes into effect.

Away from the leisure centres in the wider field of holidays and days out, changes in fashion are just as surprising. The list of innovations – water worlds, western worlds, bird and butterfly worlds, garden worlds and sea worlds, for example – is far too lengthy to detail here, but we shall take a closer look at new ideas in Chapter 6.

However, just two examples will illustrate the process by which current interests and preoccupations as featured in the media, effect the thinking and planning of leisure attractions. A wave of 'green' is sweeping across the Western world. Everywhere someone is extolling the virtues of being environmentally friendly and reducing the use of fossil fuels. In the early 1970s, the Centre For Alternative Technology was set up in the hills of Wales to demonstrate renewable energy systems, and to stimulate awareness of the wider related issues. The Centre took shape very slowly and was opened to the public in 1975. Since the onset of 'green fever', it has grown into a major tourist attraction, and development plans are being made to cater for double the present number of visitors. Research work and educational courses are conducted and there are interactive (hands-on) displays. A brochure (printed on recycled paper) lists features such as solar, wind and water-power plants, organic gardens, energy-saving houses, a vegetarian restaurant, and a bookshop which stocks a wide range of environmental books and green products.

Research has shown that 'green' concerns have performed better than the stock market average over the past few years. The Industrial Revolution has ended and the 'Environmental Revolution' is beginning, so the following story is both entrepreneurally exciting and environmentally satisfying.

A second example is the Derbyshire health spa. While drilling for

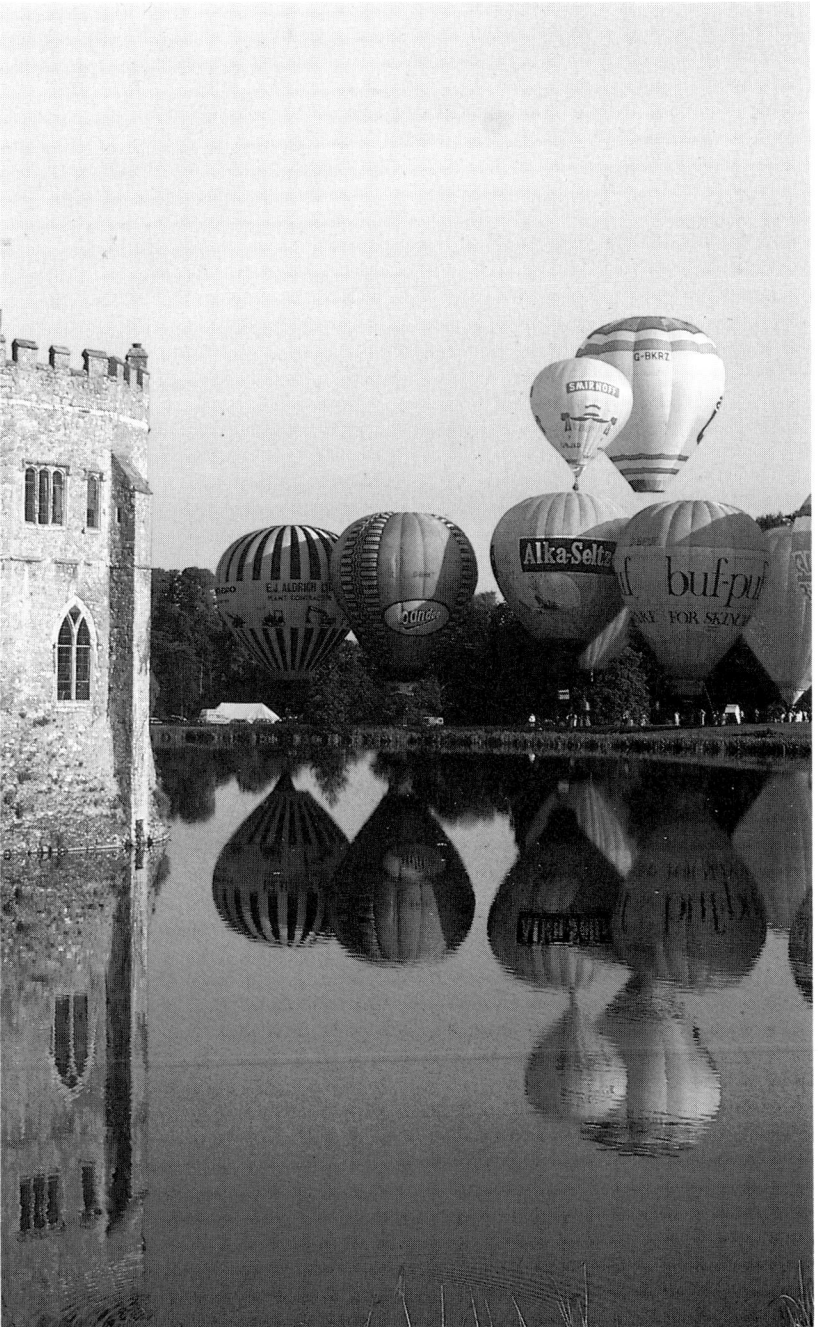

A new and innovative way of attracting the public to both a new sport and an historic venue.

(Courtesy of the Leeds Castle Foundation.)

minerals on the edge of the Derbyshire Peak District early in 1990, mining engineers were caught unawares one day by a sudden and dramatic burst of water from out of the ground. The 'gusher' climbed 150 feet into the air and signalled the accidental discovery of one of the largest, purest mineral water resources in Europe.

This happened at a time when there was concern about the purity of water coming from the average domestic tap, and a scandal about the quality of a popular brand of French bottled water. Plans are now being prepared for the development of a major leisure facility, health spa and mineral water bottling plant in this area of Derbyshire where visitor spending is already in the region of £75 million a year, because it is close to the Peak Park which attracts 22 million tourists a year and it is within 50 miles of almost half of Britain's population. Large underwater lakes are also sources of medicinal hot, cold and sulphurous springs. These factors have initiated moves to develop a major leisure facility featuring a hotel, health spa with hot and cold waters, sulphur waters, turquoise volcanic muds for mud bathing and skin treatments, as well as sports facilities. Future plans also include beauty parlours, a first-class restaurant and terrace bars, entertainment facilities and a development of exclusive chalets. Lifts will run from the hotel directly into the caverns and grottos.

In the prevailing economic climate, it is evident that there is a powerful consumer society which is on the look out for exciting and different ways of spending time and money. Leisure professionals must watch and listen very carefully to see in which direction innovations and changing tastes are leading, so that we do not miss new commercial opportunities.

Given that we have a great number of potential clients with a wide variety of interests, skills and ambitions, we, as part of the leisure industry, must have a knowledge of the practical means by which hopes and desires can become reality.

The next two chapters look at the nature of provision and examine how the cost of funding that provision is met; how in fact, the necessary money is raised and how it is distributed.

There are many different categories of provision, but we must always bear in mind that the major providers of leisure facilities are national institutions with obligations to society, committed to promoting greater social well-being. For this reason we shall refer constantly to the crucial question posed in this chapter, 'What do the customers want?' and we shall examine the balance between the specific needs of some of the groups of consumers discussed above and the funds realistically available to meet those needs.

4 Who provides what the customer wants?

As we have seen, leisure activities and, indeed, leisure itself, have over the last 200 years been luxuries available only to a few, but there has been a general change of attitude and we are actively encouraged to pursue and enjoy fun, fitness and relaxation, to expect opportunities for the exercise of body and mind, and to regard the provision of facilities as a right rather than a privilege.

Politicians have come to perceive that a healthy, contented, educated population generates a civilised society, so various departments of central government have been set up to care for the well-being of people and the environment which they live in. Parliament has, in fact, passed laws and set up agencies and bodies to ensure that this is done efficiently. These are called statutory bodies, because their authority comes from statutes – Acts of Parliament, written laws and Royal Charters. The role of central government is to advise, help to fund and co-ordinate the efforts of the national bodies concerned with sport, leisure and recreation in the UK. We shall discuss the question of funding more fully in the next chapter, but before that we must look at provision made by the public sector (national and local), the commercial sector and the voluntary sector.

The same principles apply at local as well as national level. Local councils have been set up to organise and administer tourism, entertainments and leisure services (which include libraries, theatres, museums and concert halls as well as active sports). This is also public sector provision, but because it is non-statutory the extent and quality of services vary considerably from area to area. Some councils have been content to offer just a basic recreation service, looking after parks and swimming baths. Others have played a very considerable role in leisure provision and community care, providing indoor venues of superlative quality, hundreds of acres of parks and ambitious facilities for the use of natural resources. Such enterprising authorities have the avowed aim of caring for everyone in the community at all stages of life – from pre-school playgroup to age concern.

Leisure is a fast-growing but still evolving industry and demand continues to escalate. Wherever there is a demand for a product, private organisations will appear to suppy it. If the suppliers get it right they will flourish, the customers will be satisfied and everyone will be happy. Such provision is said to be 'consumer led' or 'market led'.

Sometimes, however, consumers do not realise what they want until something is put in front of them which is fresh and eye-catching and which arouses their interest – some commodity or service which they feel they must try. Such provision is said to be 'product led' or 'supply led'. To a certain extent, the same rules apply whether the 'product' is bottled mineral water or a 'FantaSeas Tropical Indoor Water Park', liquid detergent or hi-tech library research facilities. Marketing executives are continually racking their brains to identify emerging needs and to devise new luxuries which will become necessities.

In this sector, the providers are in business to make a living, but very few industries are able to concern themselves solely with profit and gain, or are able to disregard the well-being of their customers. This is especially so in the leisure industry where the commercial sector has to be mindful of competition and be sensitive to the demands of the 'user/choosers'. The leisure industry is, after all, a service industry.

The commercial sector covers the greatest breadth of provision in the leisure industry, including: hotels, travel companies, airlines, theme parks, entertainment complexes, theatres, sports clubs, fitness centres, garden centres, heritage centres, fairgrounds, pubs and discos, aquaria ... to name but a few. More money is spent directly by the consumer in this sector than in any other sector, and the commercial companies are usually the market leaders. It is, in fact, usual for ideas and technological innovations which have been successfully pioneered in the commercial field to be adopted by the leisure and community services departments of local authorities. Also, as we shall see, the division between private and local authority provision is becoming less clear cut, and this process will continue to accelerate rapidly during the rest of the decade.

Finally, we shall look at the contribution to leisure provision made by the voluntary sector. This is what one might call the 'grass roots' structure where the enthusiasm and effort of individuals give the most opportunities for the meaningful use of leisure time. Sports, team games and hobbies are the most obvious examples of people co-operating to pursue their interests.

Amateur football clubs, cricket clubs, athletic clubs, pony clubs, classic car clubs, tennis clubs, swimming clubs, choirs, orchestras, morris-dance groups, poetry circles and many more, are organisa-tions where people of all ages make invaluable contributions in time, money and expertise to create enjoyment for themselves and others. Unpaid secretaries, treasurers, organisers, instructors, coaches, marshalls, counsellors, producers, conductors, playleaders, are the backbone of this, the largest and most diverse sector of provision. They are the admirable people who enjoy their social life and find fulfilment in helping others.

Some of the voluntary sector organisations – the St John's Ambulance Brigade, the Scout and Guide movement or the conservation charities, for example – are large national and international bodies; others are simply groups of friends or neighbours who have formed themselves into a bowls club, gardening club or darts club. The voluntary sector often operates best at a local level because the motivating force is the same in each case – the joy found in the pursuit of the sport or pastime for its own sake. These are the genuine amateurs, the 'lovers of the game'. Of course, to call someone an amateur is not to imply that he or she is second-rate or inferior to the professionals, most of whom learned or developed their own skills as unpaid enthusiasts. Amateurs also have an important role to fulfil in the world of leisure because they are the ones who, combined into voluntary organisations, have the power to protect the integrity of a sport and act as its best ambassadors both at home and abroad.

Sometimes we seek to satisfy social needs and attain practical objectives by combining with our own kind. Groups like the Women's Institute, the Townswomen's Guild, and the Roundtable, share specialised interests and have common aims.

Individuals who share a bond of nationality, race or religion form a community of interest. Thus we find in the UK groups from Eastern Europe who form clubs to keep alive their national dance, language and folklore, while there are many West Indian associations and Asian cultural societies formed to preserve their special traditions, cultures and religious beliefs.

This vast range of voluntary activities touches the everyday lives of millions of people, who are in turn brought into contact with provision made by central government, local government and commercial interests.

It is a complex pattern of involvement and inter-dependency, so perhaps we should comment briefly on each component in turn.

Central government

Until April 1992 Britain, unlike many other countries (such as France, for instance, which has a powerful Ministry of Culture) did not have a fully established government department to look after sport, leisure and tourism. We did have Ministers of State for sport and the arts, but these were junior Ministers, and the component parts of leisure were scattered all over Whitehall under the overall control of various Secretaries of State who had cabinet rank. For example, sport, physical recreation and the arts used to be an area within the responsibility of the Department of Education and Science; historic buildings came under the Department of the Environment; tourism came under the Secretary of State for Trade and Industry; broadcasting came under the control of the Home Office.

After the 1992 General Election, John Major (a Prime Minister who has made no secret of his passion for sport and enthusiasm for the arts) set up the new Department of National Heritage. The National Heritage Secretary (a Minister with a voice in the cabinet) was David Mellor. On his appointment he gave a statement to the press which left no doubt about the Government's determination to accept much greater involvement in the whole of the leisure field:

'Britain is not a museum. It is a place of dynamism; forward looking. We want to leave our imprint on history and develop those buildings that people will see as a mark of our civilisation.'

He added that the new department:

'. . . . will punch its weight, determined that culture, heritage and sport flourish. We want a country at ease with itself; the cultural and sporting dimension is vital to that vision. There is no reason why Britain should not have a Wimbledon champion in the way that backstreet children from the West Indies can rise to their international cricket team.'

This sort of philosophy is extremely encouraging to those of us who have the interests of the leisure industry close to our hearts, and should bring about developments that we have been pressing for over a period of many years.

The new Department has already been dubbed 'The Ministry of Fun' by some, and 'The Ministry for Free Tickets' by others. Nevertheless, the new Minister will have to implement three serious reforms. The first is the new national lottery (see Chapter 5). The second is to reorganise and control the chaotic field of British heritage conservation. Third, he will have to consider the future of government broadcasting policy. The BBC's charter runs out in 1996, and the whole question of public-service broadcasting will have to be looked at again in a very different commercial climate from that in which the Corporation was originally set up. At all events, this new and rather revolutionary initiative by central government is the most exciting thing to happen in the history of our industry, and we can look forward to a new era of activity and expansion.

The Minister for National Heritage has the task of co-ordinating and advising on the work of all the major providers of leisure facilities and services, while national government also supports a number of agencies, such as the Sports Council, the Arts Council and the Countryside Commission, giving funds to them so that they in turn, can supply money to make facilities and opportunities available for people to pursue leisure activities. The government also gives some money to local authorities and makes grants to parts of the voluntary sector. In addition, the planning authorities working under government control exert direct and indirect influences on commercial sector provision where the latter is concerned with developing leisure and recreational amenities. It becomes obvious then that all the suppliers of leisure opportunities are to a greater or lesser extent dependent on central government for help or approval.

Of course, whoever controls the purse-strings eventually controls policy, and we shall take a look at finance in the next chapter. But many believe that our system encourages greater input from grass-roots organisations, is less subservient and more democratic than the structures adopted by other nations.

The Sports Council is one of the most influential bodies to which the government delegates work, for it has the all-embracing duty to oversee sport in Britain. Its first and most important responsibility is set out in the Royal Charter of 1972 which confers its official status:

> To develop and improve the knowledge and practice of sport and physical recreation in the interests of social welfare and the enjoyment of leisure among the public at large in Great Britain, and to encourage the attainment of high standards in conjunction with the governing bodies of sport and physical recreation.

Although the Council depends on the Department of National Heritage for its financing, it can make decisions and act independently, even though it is stated in the Council's Charter that:

> The Council in the exercise of its functions shall have regard to any general statements on the policy of Our Government that may from time to time be issued to it by Our Secretary of State.

Although the head office of the Sports Council is in central London, its work covers the whole of England, and nine regional offices have been set up to advise and co-ordinate at a more local level. The regions are as follows:

- Northern Region (Northumberland, Cumbria, Durham, Cleveland and Tyne and Wear).
- North West Region (Lancashire, Cheshire, Greater Manchester and Merseyside).
- Yorkshire and Humberside (West Yorkshire, South Yorkshire, North Yorkshire and Humberside).
- East Midlands Region (Derbyshire, Nottinghamshire,

Lincolnshire, Leicestershire and Northamptonshire).
- West Midlands Region (West Midlands, Hereford and Worcester, Shropshire, Staffordshire and Warwickshire).
- Eastern Region (Norfolk, Cambridgeshire, Suffolk, Bedfordshire, Hertfordshire and Essex).
- Greater London and South East Region (Greater London, Surrey, Kent, East and West Sussex).
- Southern Region (Hampshire, Isle of Wight, Berkshire, Buckinghamshire and Oxfordshire).
- South Western Region (Avon, Cornwall, Devon, Dorset, Somerset, Wiltshire and Gloucestershire).
- Scotland, Wales and Northern Ireland have their own independent Sports Councils situated respectively in Edinburgh, Cardiff and Belfast.

As well as being committed to encouraging participation in, and publicising the social importance of sport, the Sports Council aims to provide the best available facilities and encourage higher standards of performance.

Towards this end, the Council has established five national 'Centres of Excellence'. These are residential sports centres which each specialise to a very high level in some aspect of sport. Primarily, the centres are intended to assist with the training of national teams and in the education of coaches, leaders and officials, but they also provide introductory courses and work with schools and the local community to increase appreciation and improve performance. These five centres are:

- Bisham Abbey National Sports Centre, Buckinghamshire, (tennis, hockey, rugby, etc.)
- Lilleshall National Sports Centre, Shropshire, (soccer, gymnastics, cricket, etc.)
- Crystal Palace National Sports Centre, Greater London, (athletics, swimming, etc.)
- Holme Pierrepoint National Water Sports Centre, Nottingham.
- Plas y Brenin National Centre for Mountain Activities, North Wales.
- Scotland, Wales and Northern Ireland also have their own National Sports Centres.

In addition to the regional offices of the Sports Council itself, there are the Regional Councils for Sport and Recreation, which sound confusingly similar. Regional Councils, however, are independent bodies which, though like the Sports Council, promote sport regionally, are also concerned with conservation, farming, forestry and tourism. The clue to their different function lies in the word

A stately setting for a centre of sporting excellence. The Lilleshall National Sports Centre, near Newport, Shropshire.

(Photograph Dave Wallace.)

'Recreation' included in the title, because as well as dealing with sport-related educational and promotional matters through the schools and clubs in their area, the Regional Councils bring together interested parties from local authorities, government ministries and departments (such as Agriculture and Trade), government agencies (such as the Forestry Commission), charitable trusts (such as the National Trust) and the people who actually own and farm the land. These useful bodies are democratic forums which have a great part to play in the management of the environment.

Just as we have the Sports Council with responsibility for sport, we have an Arts Council to do a similar job of organising provision, channelling funds, promoting the arts and having an influence on the nature of cultural facilities such as theatres, concert halls, museums and libraries, which are made available at national and local levels. Again, like its sister organisation for sport, the Arts Council has bodies to make the arts available in the regions, and there are 15 Regional Arts Associations which serve England, while there are again separate National Arts Councils for Scotland, Wales and Northern Ireland.

A comparable arrangement has grown up to promote and organise tourism in the UK. The Secretary of State for National Heritage is responsible for overseeing and funding the promotion of travel and tourism in Britain, and again there is a network of Regional Tourist Boards, and separate National Boards for Scotland, Wales and Northern Ireland. Until April 1990, the British Tourist Authority (BTA) looked after the job of promoting Britain all over the world and undertook the task of increasing the flow of foreign visitors, while the English Tourist Board (ETB), the Scottish Tourist Board, the Welsh Tourist Board and the Northern Ireland Tourist Board were more concerned with domestic tourism. Since 1990, the ETB and the BTA have combined to some extent and streamlined their operations in a move which led to a greater efficiency and released £4 million to be used by the Regional Boards, which were closer to local government departments and had a better knowledge of regional factors.

Local government

The quality of life in any given area depends on the quality of local government services. Like members of Parliament, local councillors are democratically elected, but unlike MPs, they do not receive payment and though they are able to claim expenses for attendance at council meetings, they are voluntary public servants who usually have jobs or businesses to attend to.

Our system of local government has grown up gradually over the centuries, and in order to gain some insight into the present situation, we should glance briefly at some of the principal changes along the way:

- Municipal Corporations Act 1835, which established the county boroughs with wide-ranging powers.
- Local Government Act 1888, which established 58 county councils to take from the magistrates control of the police and other major functions outside the county boroughs.
- London Government Act 1963, which established the Greater London Council and the 32 chartered London boroughs and the city of London.
- Local Government Act 1972, which abolished the county boroughs and some counties such as Rutland, Cumberland and Westmorland to create 47 non-metropolitan counties in England and Wales, and the two-tier system (county and district councils). It also created 36 metropolitan boroughs and six metropolitan county councils.

- Local Government (Scotland) Act 1973, which replaced 33 county councils, 201 city and burgh (sic) councils, and 193 district councils by 12 regional and island and 53 district councils.
- Local Government Reorganisation 1974, by which 44 new counties were created outside Greater London; six of these were called metropolitan areas established in heavily built-up areas such as Merseyside, S.E. Lancashire, Greater Manchester, the West Midlands, West Yorkshire and Tyne and Wear. Within the 44 new counties (38 plus six metropolitan areas), the existing boroughs were tidied up. Many bigger towns and cities retained their own identities, but many of the smaller towns were united with their surrounding rural communities.
- Local Government Act 1985, which abolished the Greater London Council and the metropolitan county councils.

In 1987, the Association of District Councils produced a document called *Closer to the People*, which outlined a single-tier system with unitary authorities replacing the existing county and district councils.

In April 1991, the Environment Secretary, considering that some of the new counties had not attracted the loyalties of local people, and the fact that outside the big urban areas, having two tiers of authority (the counties and the districts) blurs accountability, in that too few people know who is in charge, made clear his preference for single-purpose authorities.

It now seems extremely likely that the majority of authorities will be single-purpose bodies responsible for functions which are currently split between the district and the county councils. In many areas, particularly the 'shire' counties, the two-tier system had been considered wasteful, and many communities were still unwilling to accept the authorities created under the 1974 reorganisation of local government. It is considered probable that under fresh reforms (to be introduced possibly in 1994) the 'new' counties, such as Avon, Cleveland and Humberside, will be abolished. There are, however, no plans to change the system of local government in London and the metropolitan counties, which were restructured in 1985.

Unlike previous reorganisations, it is not proposed to adopt a sudden or wholesale abolition of either county or district councils. The new structure could vary from area to area and could either be based on the present counties or districts, the former counties abolished in 1974 or the old county borough councils which were centred on England's larger towns and also cities such as Bristol,

Plymouth and Hull, which were once responsible for all local services.

The outcome of all this will be of great importance to us as students of the leisure industry, because district councils have traditionally supplied the greater part of leisure needs for those living in any given area. Almost all interested parties on both sides of the political spectrum believe that unitary authorities can achieve more efficient and accountable local government that will also reflect local people's own sense of identity with the community in which they live. The single-tier system should also reduce bureaucracy and improve the co-ordination of services, which would increase quality and reduce costs.

Any move that would improve financial accountability to local taxpayers and offer the opportunity of relating the structure of local government to the wishes of the communities should be welcomed by those of us who have an interest in leisure provision.

Also encouraging in this respect are the proposals to enhance the role and status of parish and town councils. At present there are about 8,200 parish and town councils, which can have populations as small as 10 and as large as 40,000, and which exercise controls, shared with the districts, over sports facilities and open spaces among other things.

The department which would fall within our study would have some title like 'Leisure and Community Services', 'Amenities and Leisure Services', 'Recreation and Arts' or Parks and Recreation', and would be headed by a director or chief officer. At the highest level of administration, schemes facilitated by these departments might involve the planning and construction of multi-million pound pleasure palaces or shopping/leisure complexes; at parish level, councillors might debate a decision to supply lighting for an amateur drama group. Nowadays, district departments have started to call in professional private leisure and tourism consultants to help with market research and planning, and councils are now increasingly inviting co-operation and investment from commercial leisure developers and operators. The organisation and use of facilities was also looked at very carefully where county councils had several districts with their own leisure centres competing for custom across district boundaries. Because they try to do their best for those who have elected them, councils are very concerned about helping everyone in their area. Many have a 'sensitive' system of charging for the use of facilities, so that the young, the old, the disadvantaged and the unemployed often pay nothing at all.

Since the end of the Second World War, public leisure services have been increasingly and ambitiously supplied by local authorities, and policies have usually been conceived and pursued

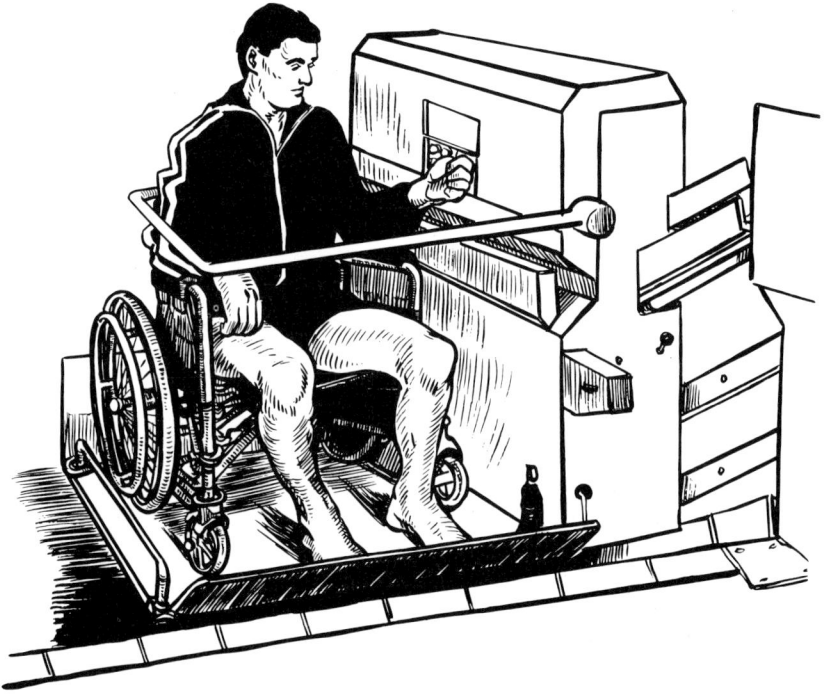

Without wheelchair lifts, the upper floors of leisure complexes and access to water chutes will be denied to disabled users.

politically. 'Service not cost' has been the motto of many councils. Take, for instance, provision for the disabled at leisure pools. There are legal requirements about access, toilets and changing rooms, but these are often considered to be an unacceptable minimum. A disabled person could ring up ahead of arrival to ask for help with opening doors and getting into the pool, but many councils now regard this as discriminatory and insist that the disabled should have their independence for, it is argued, centres should should be designed for total access at the planning stage. Details, such as unobstructed corridors, toilets and showers with plenty of room for wheelchairs, footbaths with ramps for cleaning wheelchair tyres and ramps for poolside access, should be incorporated as a matter of course. Some argue that all centres should have automatic sliding doors, extra-wide lifts should be provided to all levels, and areas in cafés and bars should be designed with tables and counters of appropriate height for wheelchair use. It is when the question of much greater expense arises that opinions are divided. For instance, a water slide is no use to disabled people if access is by a high, steep stairway. In one centre, a lift to the water slide was installed at a cost of £70,000, even though it was reasoned that there were not many disabled visitors and even fewer who might wish to ride on a water slide, but this was seen as 'The way forward in the name of greater social good.'

Very sensibly, it is often pointed out that clever design can lessen the high cost of such humanitarian provision. The lift to the water slide, for example, could be near to and on a level with other service areas for dual use, and no-one can deny that good ramps and automatic doors are a boon to the elderly, mothers with pushchairs and delivery staff, as well as the disabled.

Many councils see leisure services essentially as community services, and they offer advice, practical support and finance to self-help groups. Some councils provide 'people's centres', which are either converted or purpose-built premises containing, say, a Citizen's Advice Bureau, Job Club, resource centre, coffee bar and creche. In order to motivate the people of a district to help themselves, some councils have set up resident teams of paid community workers to work with existing voluntary organisations. The team's task is to support and start projects, as well as to provide information about council activities and services. Groups might be started for keep fit, young people, crafts, swimming, women's health and thrift shops, all on a friendly and informal basis. Sometimes newsletters are produced to keep people in touch with issues and events in the area. Money may be made available to assist with major projects, like the conversion of a building, or minor service, such as the provision of a tea urn. Council grants to voluntary groups are rarely for the whole cost of a project, because council policy is to activate volunteers into raising a proportion of the money and providing time and skills by their own efforts. This, argue the councils, is how neighbourhood spirit is fostered; it is about working together.

Grants may be given to playgroups to help with rent and equipment. An Under-Fives Forum may be established with a council-paid under-fives officer to co-ordinate the efforts of agencies like the Pre-School Play Group Association, or the National Children's Play and Recreation Unit, with voluntary playleaders and centre organisers. Lending 'libraries' of toys and large equipment are often provided by councils who, in addition, lay on social evenings at playcentres with guest speakers whose wisdom will help to improve knowledge and practice.

Play is no longer considered frivolous and time-wasting as it was a century ago, and now that it is recognised as an essential part of children's development, most urban councils provide playleadership schemes as a positive means of training the physical and mental faculties of future citizens.

Community services and leisure departments often provide summer holiday playschemes to fill up the empty days of the six-week school holidays. Trained and salaried playleaders join with unpaid volunteers to organise a programme of special events and activities. Some of the projects designed to interest, occupy and develop children of all ages and abilities might typically include drama and music workshops, clown workshops, sports tuition, arts and crafts, film shows, visits to riding schools, rock climbing and orienteering. The importance of playwork to the development of the five to fifteen age range has been finally recognised: there is now a vocational qualification for playworkers, and some councils take the service very seriously – the London Borough of Haringey, for example, has just created the post of Principal Recreation Officer in Play.

Leisure and Community Services have been linked together by some councils, partly because in an age when the number of unemployed is increasing, they see themselves as caring for a leisured society rather than one which treats free time as secondary to work. One of the interesting things about such councils is that they *never* talk about 'users' or 'the general public', but about 'customers' and 'friends'. Significantly, officials of other councils take a different point of view, reasoning that as the service is provided as a statutory duty and often provided at no cost, the term 'customer' is misleading and inaccurate.

Important as community and voluntary links are, they are often overshadowed by that local authority masterpiece – the state-of-the-art leisure complex. Over the last 20 years, local authority centres have changed dramatically; the days of bare sports halls where it was impossible to buy even a packet of crisps or a cup of tea are long over; now, many council centres are the major leisure facilities in an area. The idea of extensive (some might say lavish) facilities caught on, and currently authorities almost compete with one another to make their showpiece the biggest and best. Two examples will show the trend.

Eldon Leisure

Newcastle-upon-Tyne's Eldon Square Recreation Centre was one of the pioneers, and when its doors were opened to the public in 1976 it occupied three floors above what was, at that time, Europe's largest indoor shopping centre. It was one of the first examples of the leisure/retail mix concept, which has since become very popular. Newcastle City Council says that with about one and a quarter million admissions in 1990, it is the seventh busiest centre in Britain. It has always been progressive, with restaurant, coffee bar, multi-use sports hall, etc., but it has kept up with fashion by installing a high-tech fitness centre, sauna suite, huge, new artificial climbing wall and indoor bowling green, among other

Doncaster Leisure Park. This aerial view of part of the 350-acre leisure park shows the Dome, a major indoor leisure, sports and entertainments complex, with the most advanced facilities in Europe.
(Photograph courtesy of Doncaster Metropolitan Borough Council.)

things. It has also changed its name to 'Eldon Leisure' to reflect an updated corporate image.

The Dome

The Dome, commissioned by Doncaster Metropolitan Borough Council, was opened in 1989 after taking six years to construct, and costing £25 million. It has already been nicknamed 'the cathedral of leisure' from its resemblance to a great Renaissance church. Its architects, Faulkner Brown, describe it as: 'A high-tech structure incorporating complex technology. The traditional materials like granite and marble give it greater richness of meaning. The principal inspiration was Italian ... both Florence and Sienna have wonderful cathedrals decorated with simple banding in monochrome colours.' The leisure facilities are extensive and exciting – a two-tier ice rink with free-form ice pad of 1,500 sq m, with upper and lower levels joined by rising and falling ice ramps and surrounded by fir trees that are real (though sprayed with snow that is artificial) to create an Alpine effect.

The six section swimming complex which, as well as featuring two huge water slides, incorporates waterfalls, fountains, a 'rainbow' (made by shining lights through a curtain of water), a lazy river ride and a channel connecting to the open air. There are hydrotherapy massage jets, bubble beds and an outdoor sun terrace.

The vast sports complex combines a bowls hall, health club, snooker arcade, squash complex, functions suite and a 2,000 seater sports/events hall. Needless to say, there are imaginatively designed and sited catering facilities with bars, an associated commercial development provides a multi-screen cinema, a ten-pin bowling centre, a supermarket and a retail park. Future developments include a 60-acre lake and marina, a golf-driving-range, an indoor cricket centre and a tennis ranch. This is leisure provision on a spectacular scale. Because the site itself has already generated capital investment equal to the £25 million building cost, because energy-exchanging heating and cooling mechanisms which keep the balance between warm water and ice save fuel, costs are kept to a minimum; because takings are soaring, the whole venture is a financial and social success.

Not all councils have been so ambitious, but many local authorities have replaced their old-fashioned rectangular swimming baths with free-form leisure pools having wave machines, water rides, beach area, rockscape, tropical vegetation, etc., and 'oases', 'water palaces', 'water parks', 'lagoons', or similar water fun facilities are commonplace. These have proved very popular and successful. However, the Amateur Swimming Association has expressed concern that water play complexes are not suitable for the teaching and training of serious swimming. In fact, there has been a move away from 'stand alone' facilities, and often a 50 m competition pool exists alongside the family pool.

Local authorities have become adventurous in other types of provision apart from sport. Theme parks and heritage parks are becoming enormously popular, and local councils as well as private entrepreneurs are exploiting the vogue for recreating the past. In museums, an exhibition of stationary exhibits no longer impresses visitors, nor do long, learned lectures or printed material hold their attention. Some art galleries and museums enliven their exhibitions with sound and light shows, others issue pre-recorded information in several languages and supply either portable cassette players or earphones which are tuned into the exhibits, to each person on entry.

Others go even further. The Jorvik Viking Centre in York transports clients around in people movers, like cultural ghost-trains. Victorian parks are often seen by local authorities as fair game for development, and Brent Council, for example, produced plans to turn its Gladstone Park at Willesden, north London, into a fun world with outdoor animated models, a giant aquarium with underwater walk through tunnels, a butterfly and an orchid house, all under the name of a nature theme park.

Even an institution as respectable as Birmingham Council's City Museum and Art Gallery runs a 'Dinosaurs Alive!' exhibition. To achieve this display, animatronics experts have worked with paleontologists to blend cinema images and technical skill with scientific accuracy to show how dinosaurs lived in their environment. Life-size models that can run, feed, fly and fight are brought to life through electronic wizardry to bring the visitor 'Face to face with moving, roaring, giant dinosaurs'. We may ask ourselves if this is education or Disneyland, but the answer of the organisers would be that it is profitable business.

More restrained are the interactive displays that are increasingly being introduced into museums, where visitors can get 'hands-on' experience and make things happen for themselves. Novel types of presentation are becoming popular, and just as water fun facilities have swept the country, who is to say that animated 'jungle trails', 'adventure safaris' and 'voyages' into the past or the future will not soon be mandatory for every display at a theme park or cultural centre? Local authorities and, in particular, those with historical connections or in seaside resorts, see the commercial developers prospering on new attractions and are not averse to generating income in similar ways on their own account.

Cardiff, for instance, decided that tourism offered big rewards for the future and in 1988 launched a development programme which will continue until 2003. The City Council believes that Cardiff should: 'Draw on and borrow unashamedly from its national heritage, marketing the city along the lines of – "Cardiff, Capital of Wales, the land of Dylan Thomas, harp music, choirs, Ivor Novello ..."' The thinking of this city, which has already developed the Cardiff Bay Water Sports/Shopping/Entertainment Centre and a World Trade Centre, gives us an insight into the directions in which progressive councils are heading.

The promotion of tourism by local authorities should, nevertheless, be kept in perspective. There is always a danger of change solely for the sake of change and no-one wants that. It is worth remembering that most local authorities maintain a museum of some kind, and, indeed, in areas of historical importance there are many very valuable museums and sites which are legacies of a proud past. We must take care that our heritage is preserved, not re-invented and that quality, academic research and authoritative display techniques are not swept away in the fantasy leisure boom.

The commercial sector

As we have indicated, the local government sector and the commercial sector already work closely together. The two sectors are in the same business although with differing aims; one of them to make a profit and keep its shareholders happy (the commercial sector); the other to use the sums raised by local taxes and supplemented by central government help to provide a social service to the population, while preserving the integrity and traditions of the area (local government). It is often to the big leisure companies that councils turn when seeking advice. And, of course, it is local government planning authorities who must scrutinise the proposals of leisure companies to assess the impact of new development on the environment and its effect on the lives of local residents. In order to obtain planning permission, developers often have to include in their package schemes for community centres and low-cost housing, as well as guaranteeing a financial contribution to the cost of new road systems to reduce the adverse effects of increased traffic flow. Wherever there is expansion, re-modelling, upgrading or change of use, planning approval from the local authority is the first step.

When any leisure development is contemplated, people in the area where it is to be sited will be most concerned about the effect on their lives. In the past, uncontrolled urbanisation, particularly in popular coastal and countryside areas, brought ecological destruction and pollution of land, air and water. Large-scale tourist development or the construction of a massive leisure attraction can have an adverse effect on local culture, arts and crafts, traditional social structures and customs. For instance, when picturesque small towns and villages, stretches of coast or tracts of beautiful countryside are turned over to leisure and tourism, the whole nature of a place is irretrievably altered. People and traffic flood into the area, incongruous and hasty building development is sanctioned, and there is often a loss of identity among the local community. Problems are acute, for instance, in small Cornish villages, which have had their identities transformed, or in the Lake District, which has had to fight a constant battle against pressure from numbers of tourists which are too great to be accommodated on its roads, over-saturating its small centres of population and even eroding the hills. When an area plays host to tourist development, sensitivity is essential or the visitors will destroy the very things which they came to find. In the Mediterranean, unplanned ribbon development of the coastline with ugly concrete buildings has driven away the tourists for whom the development was undertaken.

It is to be hoped that the mistakes of the past few decades will be avoided in the future. It does seem unlikely that we should ever again allow the shoddy, jerry-built developments and tatty amusement arcades which disfigured so much of the south coast of England; such exploitation would not meet with public approval, nor would it be likely to attract trade. This is the green age, and the average member of the public is well-informed and concerned about the environment and the forces which threaten it. Planners are learning that leisure seekers are concerned about the whole of the natural world, and have more educated tastes in leisure pursuits than their forefathers. So, exhibiting concern for the environment and working in harmony with nature makes good business sense, as well as winning the approval of the official bodies of national and local government.

Center Parcs

An example of good practice which is in line with current thinking illustrates the points just covered. Center Parcs, a multi-national leisure company which has holiday villages in Holland, Belgium and France, came into the British holiday market and opened villages at Sherwood Forest in 1987 and Elveden Forest in 1989. Its enterprise, both here and on the Continent, has had great commercial success, partly because they provide high-quality villas tastefully built in natural stone, and partly because it offers a wide range of all-weather facilities. What particularly appeals to families are the water fun complexes, where children can play safely at sub-tropical temperatures surrounded by exotic vegetation, while their parents can relax in the Continental atmosphere of an open square surrounded by a variety of restaurants and shops. The villages are each sheltered by a huge transparent dome or pyramid within which the climate is carefully controlled, making the facilities usable all year round. The range of sports and games, both land and water based, is unusually wide and imaginative. As well as being ideal for active and adventurous pursuits the villages, because they are set in almost 500 acres of natural countryside, give scope for gentle pastimes, such as walking, fishing or just peaceful relaxation.

The greatest strength of the Centre Parcs concept, however, is that the villages, far from spoiling the rural environments in which they are located, actually enhance and improve them. The villas are made to blend into the environment by being constructed of natural materials and being placed into a well afforested and contoured landscape. For centuries water has been recognised as essential to

The lake at Center Parcs Sherwood Forest Village where equipment is available for sailing, windsurfing and canoeing. In the background can be seen the huge futuristic dome which encloses the water play facilities.

(Photograph courtesy of Center Parcs.)

any ideal landscape. Not only is water beautiful and restful, it is also the focal point of most outdoor recreation. Centre Parcs has brought water to areas where it did not naturally occur, so by the use of channels, waterfalls and lakes it has improved the habitat of the native flora and fauna, and added a new aspect to the area to delight our senses.

On arrival, cars are left on a car park and guests go peacefully around the meadows and woodlands either on foot or by bicycle. The proof that this green approach appeals to today's holidaymakers is seen in fact that occupancy of accomodation at the holiday villages runs at over 95 per cent. Here then, is the evidence that commercial sector leisure provision need not be intrusive in areas of natural beauty.

The Hospitality Industry

Hotels too are changing in response to the fashion for fitness, and it is now quite common to see a notice reading, for example: 'Radbrook

Hotel and Leisure Centre. Fitness Suite and Sauna.' Such extra facilities which were once unknown in hotels give businessmen and women as well as tourists and holidaymakers the opportunity to relax or tone up. Formerly, television and bars were the only attractions on offer. This is changing rapidly and the trend is away from hotels, as 'stand alone' facilities, towards 'residential leisure parks'. An example of this is Kenwick Hall near Louth in Lincolnshire. It was bought by a group of businessmen who spent £10 million on a scheme which includes a 100 bedroom hotel, a 24-lane golf driving range, timeshare, owner-occupied and rented properties. In addition, the 200-acre site has a 12-acre lake for angling and watersports, a swimming pool and horse riding facilities, an 18-hole golf course and parking for 100 touring caravans.

The 'sports village' is a similar type of private development, where a hotel with, say, 150 beds provides accommodation, while on site there are indoor tennis courts, squash courts, snooker tables, gym, sauna, health club, multi-purpose sports hall, a 25 m swimming pool and a leisure pool. Outdoors there is a golf driving range, tennis courts, hockey pitch and cricket ground. These 'villages', which have restaurants, bars and retail outlets, are open to the general public on a 'pay and play' basis without membership fees, and the management also runs sports courses with professional tuition. Two of these developments at Norwich and Chigwell, near Epping, are proving popular, and it is likely that this type of integrated development, grouped either round a hotel or self-catering cottages and studios will be the pattern for the future of commercial leisure complexes. Many more health related leisure ventures exist all over the British Isles with spas and health hydros springing up again as they once did in the last century.

New-style hotels with pools and fitness centres and sports facilities are also being built at an increasing rate near ports, airports and exhibition centres. Golf courses have traditionally had their related hotels nearby, but now the tendency is for new golf courses (which are coming into commission at a startling rate), to stand alongside hotels or self-catering units, surrounded by multi-sports facilities.

Taking part in sport does cost money, but people willingly pay to follow their interests, and as more municipal sports and leisure facilities are being brought into the private sector, increased customer flow and competition mean that prices are coming down.

Sponsorship

It seems natural that manufacturers of sporting goods and clothing should sponsor team games, and that travel companies should sponsor skiing championships, but there are companies in the commercial sector who are not directly associated with leisure, but are large-scale providers of funds for sport, recreation and the arts. In 1990, the sponsorship market was worth £288 million, and the activities covered ranged from snooker through classical music to caring for the environment. Association with events or causes that catch the public's imagination is a very beneficial and effective form of advertising. As funding from central and local government is cut or frozen, sponsorship can provide the support needed to keep sport and the arts alive, and provide opportunities to reduce costs to the public. So effectively has this arrangement worked over the last decade that we are all familiar with events such as the Lombard RAC Rally, the Rumbelow's Football Cup, the Cornhill Insurance Cricket Tests, and the Whitbread Around the World Yacht Race. Such popular national events have proved to be cost-effective promotional devices, which have worked to the benefit of all concerned.

Classical music, opera and ballet events are extremely expensive to stage, and cuts in government subsidies mean that the prices of tickets for arts events have soared far above the rate of inflation. The result of this is that fewer people can afford to attend live performances, and revenue from ticket sales has fallen sharply in spite of increasing interest in cultural programmes. Great orchestras, such as the London Symphony Orchestra, are struggling, the expansion and refurbishment of London's famous Royal Opera House has led to urgent appeals for voluntary contributions from opera lovers, while classical dance companies, such as the Royal Ballet and the English National Ballet, have found themselves in financial difficulty. Without sponsorship the situation would be even worse, and various degrees of ingenuity are employed by artistic directors in the quest for funds.

An example of determination shows what can be done. In 1990 the Northern Ballet Theatre was driven from Manchester to Halifax by local authority funding cuts, and to avoid further financial troubles in their new location, the ballet company appealed to the public of Halifax. Every piece in the dancers' wardrobe was offered for sponsorship. Among others, a department store, a clothing company and a hairdressing partnership all put up money, but, more unusually, hosts of ordinary people from all walks of life were invited to do the same. Gifts from £10 to £250 flooded in, and the result was a lavish production which won both popular and professional critical acclaim. This public spirited form of sponsorship leads us naturally to consider the final sector of provision – the voluntary sector.

The voluntary sector

As far as sport is concerned, the principal organisation to be considered is the Central Council of Physical Recreation (CCPR). This greatly respected independent voluntary body has within it the representatives of more than 240 governing bodies of sport and physical and recreational activities. It was formed in 1935 as an enthusiast's organisation to promote and encourage sport, and nowadays its work covers more than 87,000 affiliated local sports clubs with literally millions of individual members. These governing bodies are themselves important, as they make, regulate and enforce the rules of sports and activities right up to national and international levels. The CCPR is very concerned about the image of sport, and part of its task is to act as a public relations body which realises that violence and hooliganism, cheating and the use of drugs, racism and vandalism all damage the public estimation of what should be healthy and life-enhancing activities.

In the pursuit of sporting excellence, the CCPR also co-operates with the Sports Council and the British Olympic Association. The CCPR's own guide explains simply what it does:

> As the collective voice of sport, the CCPR relates the views of the governing bodies to the Government, the Sports Council, local and other authorities, to each other and to the nation. The CCPR is the national voice of sport and recreation in this country. The CCPR serves the governing bodies. It is their organisation and their voice.

The government plans to re-organise sport to make one unified body to replace the CCPR, the Sports Council and the British Olympic Association, but there are many who believe that the CCPR with its genuine love of the game attitude, its guardianship of fair play and its resistance to commercialism in sport is an indispensable, informed forum that must be retained.

A splendid example of professionals combining with amateurs to promote the image and enjoyment of a game is given by the Football in the Community Programme, managed and operated by the Professional Footballers Association (the players' union). This scheme establishes contacts with amateur clubs, schools, youth clubs and the probationary service. Professional players, officials and former players give coaching sessions in soccer and cricket, give talks at local community meetings and promote sports-related activities. The aim is to make more use of the excellent facilities of professional clubs to foster interest in the game, while involving ethnic, minority and disadvantaged groups in other social and recreational pursuits. The players and officials give their time generously in the knowledge that they are also helping to reduce the incidence of anti-social behaviour often associated with football. More than thirty league clubs are currently involved in the scheme and there are plans for its further expansion.

We have looked at this example from the world of soccer because it is still the most popular team game, with over two million players, but we must remember that it is not just in the area of sports and games that the combination of volunteers and highly skilled professionals may frequently be observed as a positive force for good in the community. Voluntary support groups undertake a vast range of activities and help make life more fulfilling and enjoyable for the volunteers and others. Some individuals choose to devote their leisure to helping the sick by joining the League of Friends of local hospitals; others work as volunteer wardens in the National Parks to protect the landscape, or form themselves into rescue teams to save the lives of those in trouble in wild tracts of countryside. Keen fishermen supplement the work of water bailiffs, and members of the 77,000 strong Ramblers' Association tramp tirelessly to keep footpaths open and campaign for the conservation of beauty spots and wild life habitats threatened by urbanisation. Amateur engineers and engine drivers work for long hours at weekends and during holidays so that old steam trains may puff and snort for the delight of the tourists which they transport on private railway lines during the summer months.

No archaeological dig would be possible without a team of enthusiasts spending long hours in the delicate and skilled work of sifting the soil an inch at a time. The picture is the same in industrial archaeology – the Ironbridge Gorge Museum has become one of the world's great sources of information about the Industrial Revolution through the co-operation of enthusiasts and academic historians, for example. There are magazines and journals that detail the work and cater for the interests of amateurs in almost any field that one can think of, and the educational value of the work done by loyal disciples and helpers is beyond calculation. Of great importance, too, is the fact that a large and organised group of enthusiasts constitutes a pressure group, which can become so powerful that no political party would be wise to ignore its voice, as may readily be appreciated by looking at the strength of the green lobby at home and abroad.

Voluntary organisations are always seeking ways of increasing their income and spreading the taste for their particular interests, and clubs which at one time would have kept their facilities purely for their members are now opening them up to the general public. This is especially evident in air sports, such as ballooning, gliding, parachuting, hang-gliding and flying, where weekend or holiday programmes generate funds and encourage new members. Many of the new clubs which are springing up in response to the golf boom offer similar introductory 'play and see' schemes, which they make available during holiday periods, for no sport can be kept exclusive without the risk of ignoring or stifling up-and-coming talent.

The National Trust

Before concluding this overview of the voluntary sector, let us take a look at one of the largest charitable trusts, the National Trust. There are many other voluntary organisations associated with the provision of leisure and recreational facilities, but the Trust is perhaps the best known. For almost a hundred years, the Trust has worked for the preservation of places of historic interest and natural beauty in England, Wales and Northern Ireland (there is a separate National Trust for Scotland). The properties of the Trust cannot be sold or mortgaged and so are preserved for the enjoyment of the public from generation to generation. The Trust's handbook gives a full picture of its scope and range:

> Today the Trust — which is not a government department but a charity depending on the voluntary support of the public and its members — is the largest private landowner and conservation society in Britain. Wherever you go you are close to land that is protected and maintained by the National Trust. 460 miles of unspoilt coastline (more than a third of the finest that remains); nearly 600,000 acres of fell, dale, lake and forest (140,000 in the Lake District alone); prehistoric and Roman antiquities ranging from Hadrian's Wall to the Cerne Giant in Dorset; downs and moorlands, fens, farmlands, woods and islands; nature reserves; lengths of inland waterway — even all or the greater part of 44 villages — are open to the public at all times subject only to the needs of farming, forestry and the protection of wildlife.
>
> The Trust also protects more than 100 gardens and about 200 historic buildings which it opens to visitors. Castles and abbeys, houses of architectural or historic importance, tithe barns, mills, gardens and landscaped parks have been given to the Trust by their former owners. ... Many houses retain their original contents of fine furniture, pictures and other treasures accumulated over the generations.

Just how great a contribution the Trust makes to people's enjoyment of leisure may be estimated by the fact that there are about eight million visitors to its properties every year.

There are also National Trust Associations and Centres which have developed over the last 30 years. These are autonomous groups of Trust members, varying in size from 100 to 2,000, whose purpose, as well as raising funds and recruiting new members, is to organise visits to properties, lectures and social events. National Trust Volunteer Groups and Young National Trust Groups undertake practical work for the Trust and encourage young people to join the Trust and take an active interest in its work as well as organising 'Acorn Camps' for children under 16. Trust members are often invited to act as voluntary wardens, stewards and lecturers at Trust properties which increases their own involvement, and helps this admirable organisation to continue its work of conservation and education.

The four sectors which we have briefly examined are all part of a partnership between a network of agencies, public and private, amateur and professional, which are working together towards a common aim – to provide encouragement, facilities and opportunities for every individual in Britain, irrespective of age, ability or background, to enjoy a happier and healthier life.

5   Who pays the bill?

The short answer to this question is: the customer, client or consumer. We all pay for what we get and, sometimes, with luck, we get what we pay for. Having said that some people do undoubtedly pay more than others for the use, enjoyment and even the existence of leisure facilities, but we all pay something whether in point-of-entry charges, national taxation (income tax, VAT, etc.) or local taxes such as the council tax. Not everyone likes paying taxes, whether national or local, for amenities which they themselves may not use or want, as evidenced by this letter written to the local press by 'Disgruntled Taxpayer':

> We need education and social services, but have our councillors thought of planting fewer daffodil bulbs or rose bushes, or the possibility of refraining from spending our money on revamping the Shirehall forecourt or the reception area? These items are pretty, but do we need them?
>
> Also, surely more could be done to ensure that council owned facilities are NOT run at a loss, at our expense?
>
> For instance, losses on the Music Hall mean that I (and hundreds of others) subsidise the entrance fees for the various entertainments shown there (which very few people attend).
>
> And why should I (through my local taxes) help to pay for the pleasure of people using the council owned sports centres yet, if my leisure activity happens to be bowling, using a rowing or motorboat, cinema going or attending a disco I am (quite rightly) expected to pay the full cost?
>
> I do pay my local taxes, but very reluctantly, because I know that a considerable portion of it will be spent on non-essentials.

'Disgruntled' no doubt thinks that he or she has got something of a point, but shows a lack of appreciation of the needs of others by phrases such as 'at our expense', and 'why should I . . . help pay for the pleasure of people', and begs a lot of questions with the reference to 'non-essentials'.

In an ideal world, people would have enough money to pay for their own pleasures and relaxations, but in the real world there will always be those who are very short on spending power and yet have many needs, and who, without subsidies from central and local funds, would have few opportunities for the exercise of body or mind. Perhaps if 'Disgruntled' read the earlier chapters of this book, he or she would see what life could be like without facilities for recreation and the arts, and how bleak life might be without a few civic daffodils and roses. The whole concept of a community is founded on appreciating the needs and fulfilling the aspirations not of just oneself, but of one's neighbours as well.

It is not just members of the public who are opposed to the concept of leisure being made available to all, as the following newspaper item clearly illustrates. The real names of the area and of the speakers have been omitted, otherwise, like the letter reprinted above, it is a transcript of an actual item quoted just as it appeared in a regional newspaper.

Price Tag on Leisure is Target for Attack

A member of the district council claims that the council's leisure centres are costly white elephants, and another says there is increasing opposition to the cost of leisure services, but this has been denied by the council vice-chairman. Councillor Brown told a general purposes committee meeting: 'We are spending all this money subsidising leisure centres used by a minority of people in the district.' He said centres were making losses of up to £150,000 and asked: 'How can you justify this to people within the district? These white elephants are becoming increasingly more expensive.'

Councillor James told the committee: 'There is an upsurge of opposition to the cost of leisure centres. You can't deny that.' But Councillor Smith said: 'They are not white elephants.' And the council treasurer said that virtually all councils subsidised leisure facilities. 'But this council has taken the view that charges should be on a level which would minimise that subsidy,' he said. He added that European grants towards the cost of building centres demonstrates support for leisure policies. The council chief executive also said that the council was proposing a reduction in the cost of leisure services. The technical services director said more than 200,000 people used the town leisure centre in 12 months, and it was estimated that more than 300,000 would use the new county centre in a full year.

Some idea of how costs could be kept down may be gained from considering the answers given by John Trower, Leisure Services Area Manager for South Wrekin, to a few queries about funding:

We are now in the game of generating income as quickly as we can. The only alternative is cutting services, because we have to balance our books; we are accountable. We have to do more new things now to make sure that people keep on coming back to us. We do new things, even if we have to accommodate fads – short mat bowling, fitness testing, soft play areas, whatever. In the past the local authority did not allow response time for us to be quick. Now we have to be quick. We have business plans for each area of the site.

When asked about the vexed question of subsidising some customers more than others, he was remarkably honest:

The government is now ensuring that. The complaint was that subsidies weren't targeted and didn't reach the people who needed them, and there was an element of that. Now we write down the type of customers we have, who they are, what they like, and what they don't like; we have to talk to them and create a whole stockpile of information.

Our research shows that 80 per cent of our users come from social groups A, B, and C, so we have to operate our concession scheme so that it really does hit those who need it . . . and we do. Those who need to go swimming free – and everything else, except the ski slope – right across our area.

As the result of sensitive pricing policies many local authorities leisure centres offer parent and child swimming sessions at a nominal fee.

(Photograph Dave Wallace.)

As we have seen in earlier chapters, leisure, politics and society are all intermixed; public preoccupations and economic conditions constantly alter our attitudes towards leisure. For instance, a survey by Mintel, the market analysts, estimated that in 1990 people spent £80.7 billion on housing, and they estimated that by the year 2000, 80 per cent of the population will own their own homes, as opposed to 67 per cent in 1990 and 56 per cent in 1980. Bearing this in mind, one does not have to be an economist to see that any rise in the mortgage rate would bring about a massive cutback on luxuries for the majority of home owners ... and expenditure on leisure might then be perceived as an extravagance. On the other hand, as people become more fitness-conscious, a healthy lifestyle with plenty of exercise is not now regarded as a luxury, but as an enjoyable necessity which is an essential preparation for advancing years. Both these factors affect people's attitudes to how they spend their leisure and their money.

Government funding

Let us take another example of changing social conditions affecting the amount of money spent on leisure provision. For over a decade now there has been anxiety about the decline of city life and the breakdown of community spirit, which in turn can lead to poor health, rising crime figures and civic unrest. This is often put down to homelessness and unemployment, but it has also been realised that lack of leisure facilities aggravates the problem.

In 1990, £4 billion was spent on the City Action Budget, but that amount has increased yearly by means of injections of funds from central government and the responsibility for the scheme has been upgraded from junior minister to cabinet level.

This sort of initiative was encouraged by the success of the 1980s campaign in Liverpool by which an alliance of the private and public sector brought about an inner city revival, and won high praise from all concerned. The expression 'inner city' has now been replaced by 'urban regeneration', so that concern can be widened to the problems of sprawling housing estates that border city centres.

Generosity can also be shown to individual institutions as in the case of the Ironbridge Gorge Museum Trust, which in 1992 received £4 million from the government because it is 'one of the great museums of the world'. This generosity was partly encouraged by the fact that the Museum has a Development Trust which is raising £1 million per annum through sponsorship and undesignated gifting (money that can be used wherever need is greatest rather than on specific projects).

Hand-outs from central government are not always enough to

ensure the survival of great institutions, as the troubled recent history of London Zoo clearly shows. In 1988, the government gave £10 million to London Zoo to safeguard its future, but then the sum required escalated to over £40 million, and the government was not prepared to give more cash until businessmen and conservationists showed willingness to finance exhibits and events. Offers of private intervention led in turn to hostility from local people who feared it might become a 'Disney World' operation.

Sometimes, when juggling financial resources, a government can raise money for one political initiative, only to deprive another area of the benefits it already enjoys – in other words, 'rob Peter to pay Paul'! An example of this occurred when in 1991 VAT was raised by 2.5 per cent to 17.5 per cent to reduce the burden of local taxation. One unforseen result of this move was that theatre tickets became more expensive, and that the Royal Shakespeare Company and the English National Opera, for instance, were faced with the difficult alternative of increasing prices by passing on the VAT to the customer (thus pricing out patrons), or losing hundreds of thousands of pounds by absorbing the extra cost. It has been estimated that the rise in VAT could cause a loss of £10 million to theatres nationally, and that inevitably, some might have to close. The same unenviable situation of course, faces all other entertainment venues, theme parks, leisure attractions, etc., whether subsidised or not.

Not all social and financial changes, however, are for the worse – consider the new National Lottery. For years social and religious opinion in Britain opposed the notion of a state lottery, although these are common in Europe. With progress towards a common European policy and a single European market, it became likely that we would be swamped by thousands of lottery tickets from foreign countries, so a National Lottery appeared to be a matter of common sense. The weekly prize for the lucky ticket holder will be £1 million, and annual ticket sales should raise £3 billion, one billion of which will be set aside for environment and arts projects. Lottery grants will go towards major refurbishment work to national museums and art galleries, including the British Museum, National Gallery and Natural History Museum; London theatres, galleries and historic landmarks are also considered for a share of the proceeds.

This initiative goes hand in hand with a scheme from the private sector by which the football pools promoters contribute £40 million from pools receipts to a Foundation for Sport and the Arts. The government makes available a further £20 million by a 2.5 per cent reduction in pools betting duty. The Foundation, which provides a substantial boost to the funding of both sport and the arts, is administered by a trust.

Local authority funding

When looking at the structure of provision for leisure and recreation in the last chapter, we noted that central government, acting through its ministries and departments, provides funds for agencies like the Sports Council and the Arts Council. Generally speaking, this money comes from national taxes and schemes, such as the ones outlined above. We have seen central government also gives cash to local authorities, so that they can provide leisure and other services to the people within their area. To help with financing its own projects and providing its services, each local authority raises more funds by imposing local taxes. This is the area of finance that causes most controversy and prompts many letters like the one with which we began this chapter. One reason for this is that people see that they are being asked to make a bigger contribution than their neighbours, even when they make less use of facilities. This is why rates (a property-based tax collected until 1990) were so unpopular, as they varied considerably from one property to the next and were seen as unfair. The Community Charge, or Poll Tax (a flat-levy collected between 1990 and 1992), was positively hated by most people mainly because, through its insistence of the principle that all should contribute, it put heavy burdens on those least able to pay. The Council Tax (property based, and banded) is more work-able and easily collectable.

Many people resent local taxes, whatever their form, because they are not always related to what are considered to be 'essentials', and also because we can see for ourselves the results of local authority expenditure immediately – see things happening on our own door-steps, as it were. It is all a matter of values, of approving of what the money is spent on, and then perceiving value for money – seeing schemes as worthwhile and being shown that the tax paid goes as subsidies to those who really need it. That is why the structure of local government has been more closely related to the wishes of the community ... made more local, in fact, and attempts have been made to sort out the tangle of council finances.

However, local residents in any given area pay only 28 per cent of local bills. The fact is then, that the greater part of council finance comes straight from central government in the form of grants and the Business Rate. The latter is set and levied centrally (on a national basis and returned to local authorities on a population basis). It is only increased in line with inflation, so that it follows that if the grant is not increased or even reduced, the authority is faced with providing a lower level of service or adding to the localist tax bill. This is the process known as 'capping'.

Three major factors will govern the extent of local authority provision for some time to come. Firstly, the overall financial constraints on council spending outlined above. Secondly, the rising affluence of the majority of consumers. Thirdly, the political decision to encourage greater competition within the established area of local authority operation.

Tightening of the purse-strings will mean that on-site generated income must be kept at maximum level. That consideration is very real; consider the fact that in the first six years of the 1980s, government restrictions on local government resulted in a fall of central financial support from 66 per cent to 49 per cent. This means that equipment and premises must now be used to the full, 'making every minute pay'. In turn, this means that everyone practising in the leisure industry is under pressure both from legislation (an Act to enforce competition became law in 1989), and higher customer expectation, but and also because of rising competitive standards.

Compulsory competitive tendering

This has led to the situation known as compulsory competitive tendering (CCT). Under this approach to local government services, district councils have an 'enabling role'. This means that councillors would attempt to estimate what the local community would require in terms of facilities and provision, and then, rather than automatically fulfilling that need themselves, they would invite private companies to bid for the right to provide these services for a specified period. Councils would also put in their own bids for the right to provide these services through a direct service organization (DSO); a contract would be awarded on the basis of cost-effectiveness. Many councils would make great efforts to put in efficient 'in-house bids' to ensure the continuation of their social and political philosophies. Local authorities have always felt that they should be able to spend local taxes as they please, while central government has always felt that its payment of large grants gives it the right to interfere. Perhaps CCT is the answer to this conflict of interest, ensuring that the customer gains as money is more efficiently spent. By 1 January 1993, 100 per cent of sport and leisure is subject to tendering.

This is, of necessity, a very brief outline of the CCT situation, so perhaps a glance at an actual invitation for tenders (opposite) will make the process clearer.

History was made in January 1991 in North Wales when Delyn Borough Council became the first local authority to win the contract for the management of its own sports and leisure facilities. As Delyn Leisure Management, an in-house contractor, the borough team faced stiff competition from two private companies under the terms of CCT. The contract initially covered a six-year period and related to all leisure facilities in the areas of Flint, Holywell and Mold. Perhaps there will be fewer 'Disgruntleds' in this region as services

BRISTOL CITY COUNCIL
Select List of Tenderers
Local government Act 1988

(Competition in Sport and Leisure Facilities Order 1989)

In accordance with the provisions of the Local Government Act 1988, Bristol City Council intends to invite tenders for the management of sports and leisure facilities and applications are invited from contractors who wish to be considered for inclusion on a select list of tenderers.

The contract will be for four years commencing January 1992 for the management of Easton Leisure Centre, Horfield Sports Centre, Kingsdown Sports Centre, Robin Cousins Sports Centre and Whitchurch Sports Centre.

are established on a competitive basis and the use of existing facilities is maximised.

Realistic pricing should also leave more resources for the benefit of disadvantaged people – those on very low incomes, students and disabled people, for example. These groups will always exist as a minority, but a substantial minority; and just as there are always those who are affluent enough not to be affected too much by rising prices, there will always be those who do not share in this affluence, so the burden is going to fall more heavily on the average customer, with only genuine cases of need having free or very cheap services. With realistic management of local taxpayers' money, there might even be some funds left over for amenity horticulture to improve the quality of life for everyone in the district; after all, it was early municipal legislation on parks and open spaces which made the breakthrough to a better way of life in the dark days of the nineteenth century.

Before we become too gloomy about the money available to local authorities, we should remember that conditions change rapidly and dramatically from time to time, and alter the whole scenario – so, for that matter, do political influences and ideologies. In any event, important though local authority funding is, it is only a small proportion of the total of leisure spending. These figures, taken from the *Report of the Henley Centre for Forecasting (1991)*, speak for themselves. Total Value of UK Leisure Market, £72.5 billion. Consumer spending on local authority services in England and Wales, £250 million. Total Council Rate expenditure by councils, £1 billion. This can leave us in no doubt that the private sector plays the leading role in the British leisure industry.

Let us look at a few examples of domestic spending in the commercial leisure market. Theme parks are flourishing currently with total payments for admission in 1991 standing at £108 million. A theme park is defined as an attraction which is built around one or more fantasy or historical theme, charges some form of all-inclusive entry fee and offers a range of facilities, such as rides, playgrounds, scenic displays, some entertainment, shopping and catering, wide enough to occupy a family for a whole day. At present there are 13 major parks in Britain and the number is still growing.

In addition to these newer day trip venues, there are the traditional British seaside resorts, visits to sites of historic interest and other destinations to tempt trippers. An accurate survey conducted by the English Tourist Board (ETB) in 1991 estimates that 630

Thorpe Park is one of the 13 major theme parks in Britain today. (Photograph courtesy of Leisure Sport Ltd.)

million day trips per year by 443 million visitors generate a staggering £5.2 billion. The ETB has even more encouraging statistics relating to hotels and private health clubs, golf courses and holiday villages. The point is that we should reflect on figures like these before coming to the conclusion that cutbacks in local authority spending are seriously affecting the leisure market, and the prospects for employment of those who wish to work in it. In the final chapter, we shall look at council finance again, noting how new attitudes to marketing and partnerships are improving income.

The importance of volunteers

The voluntary sector has for many years done its share of helping out where funds for paid officials would be difficult to find. Unpaid stewards at concert and theatres, voluntary play leaders and youth workers, amateur marshalls at motorsport events, and amateur referees in Sunday league soccer matches – these and many others have played a vital part in sport and the arts for decades. Now that councils do not have enough money to do all that they would like to do, they have developed schemes to support the voluntary sector and get the general public and enthusiast groups involved. Appeals for volunteer labour and offers of advice and financial support to community groups are being put out by councils. Individuals are being asked to give their spare time to libraries, museums, the

Volunteers can achieve a huge amount and also help countryside conservation enormously.

(Photograph courtesy of A. C. Cowe.)

countryside, sport and general recreation. Hundreds of parish councils and volunteer groups are now working with the support of district councils to protect and beautify the environment so that others may enjoy it. Volunteer tree wardens, countryside rangers and wildlife conservationists are being offered free training and a chance to work with the professionals in this valuable rural initiative.

Urban areas also have their volunteers who are interested in our industrial heritage and work alongside the reclamation agencies to preserve and restore those relics which are interesting and educationally informative about the way we used to live and work. It must not be forgotten that such projects as these can also attract European Community grants and European development grants.

In situations of strict capital controls, the cash created and the efforts made by voluntary fund-raising groups is of paramount importance. A brief mention of two of the enormous number of these important organizations will give some idea of the sort of finance that can be raised by the efforts of sports enthusiasts.

The British Sports Trust works to support the training of 80,000 voluntary sports leaders. The Trust uses sport as a way of channelling the energy of young people into healthy activities, and this costs a great deal of money, so in 1991–2 the Trust's target has been to raise £3 million. Their Community Sports Leaders Award Scheme operates 2,000 courses producing 27,000 leaders to work as volunteers in youth groups, sports clubs and community associations. For this purpose, donations or covenants from commercial organisations are invited, along with subscriptions from individuals who are willing to support the idea of developing leadership skills in young people.

Having a similar aim of helping young sportsmen and women, the Sports Aid Foundation (SAF) was created for the purpose of making money available to assist individual British sportspeople to compete with distinction in the Olympic Games, World and European Championships and other international events. The SAF also has a

Steve Backley, holder of the World, European and Commonwealth javelin records. Steve was first helped in his career by a Sports Aid Foundation grant. (Photograph courtesy of Shropshire Magazine.)

regional structure that works throughout Britain to raise funds to help local youngsters who have the potential to become the champions of the future and, in addition, it gives financial support to competitors with disabilities who need to realise their sporting potential. The costs of training and travelling expenses are very high, and without the splendid work done by the SAF much national talent would be wasted. The point of having a body like the SAF is made clear when we consider some champions like Sebastian Coe, Daley Thompson, Tessa Sanderson, Duncan Goodhew, Steve Backley and Jane Torvill and Christopher Dean – all of whom were provided with SAF assistance early in their careers. From the time when it was founded in 1976, to 1990, over 2,000 sportspersons representing 49 sports had received £613,691 in grant aid. This charitable trust derives its income from a lottery, commercial sponsorship, fund-raising events and donations from companies, voluntary bodies and members of the public. Everyone connected with the trust gives his or her services free, and it is only through this sort of goodwill that this country can hope to look forward to Olympic excellence.

As we have already seen, in Chapter 4, there are many other examples of commercial sponsorship which are assuming an increasingly important role in helping to finance all forms of recreational provision. With money becoming increasingly difficult to raise and with funding causing constant problems, the work of marketing executives has become increasingly important. In the next chapter, we shall examine the way in which guidelines for leisure provision are marketed to the general public.

6 How are services marketed?

Our look at the historical background of leisure facilities showed us that in the early years, any kind of provision was eagerly seized upon and demand often exceeded supply, because there was a developing, increasingly prosperous captive market seeking new and more exciting ways of spending time and money.

The situation today is rather different, for although the number of potential customers has increased, so too has the competition for their trade. Nowadays, providers of leisure opportunities can no longer just throw open the doors of old, familiar attractions and wait for the crowds to pour in. All sectors have been affected by the rise in customer expectations in terms of quality and variety, services and environment, so that now central government departments, development corporations, local authorities, tour operators, hotel groups, and heritage companies all call in leisure consultants to make market appraisals and feasibility studies for new ventures, operational improvement studies and offer financial guidance.

In the 1990s, an understanding of marketing skills is a necessity, for we have just seen in Chapter 5 how the reality of compulsory competitive tendering, has made for re-thinking in all civic headquarters, altering the way in which municipal facilities are perceived by the public. They used sometimes to be thought of as cheap (often free), 'last resort', 'take-it-or-leave-it' services; unfortunately, in some areas this had been true.

Now, however, both local councils and certain voluntary organisations are eager to form partnerships with commercial experts so that they may come up to the high standards expected by today's consumers. Two actual advertisements (opposite) from professional journals will make this point clear.

Central government is trying to encourage commercial operators to provide services for, or alongside, local authorities at a time when entertainment, retailing, recreation and sport are being more closely linked – the term 'festive retailing' has been devised to cover the concept of shopping malls with horticultural displays and landscaping intermixed with leisure/heritage attractions, bars and restaurants. This has proved to be a popular marketing mix, and is enjoyed as much by families doing the weekly shopping as by tourists on holiday.

SANDWELL
WEST MIDLANDS
Department of Leisure
Public Golf Course Development

The Council, at a time of increasing demand, is committed to
ensuring that its two public golf courses provide a quality and
cost effective service to local golfers.

The Council's Leisure Strategy Committee has decided that a
golf course revitalisation programme should be prepared, and
has instructed the Director of Leisure to enter into discussions
with golf development companies with a view to attracting
investment and maximizing income.

A conceptual brief detailing the Council's objectives is in the
process of preparation and will be made available to companies
which express an interest and can demonstrate that their
qualifications and status make them suitable to enter into
partnership arrangements with the Council.

HERITAGE ATTRACTION OPERATOR
Cheltenham

A high-quality visitor attraction themed on spa heritage is to be
created close to the centre of Cheltenham. The concept has
been prepared by Phoenix Design. The charitable trust which
will own the attraction wishes to appoint a company to manage
and market it. This company will pay a fee to the owners in
order that the attraction can be adequately maintained and
updated, but will otherwise retain the profits from entry fees,
retail shop and limited corporate hospitality use in the evenings.

Although the attraction will not open for 18 months, the
operating company is being sought now so that it can contribute
to the final planning and design and can carry out advanced
marketing.

The demise of 'welfarism'

What we are currently witnessing is a movement away from
'welfarism', the long-established belief that civic amenities should
not be profit seeking, that community need should not be subject to

market forces. The impact of the changing economic, social and political climate is leading to the demise of welfarism, so services are becoming more customer orientated and income-generating.

The debate about the desirability of this trend is beyond the scope of this book, but there is no doubt that the general public will make up its collective mind about related changes in cost and quality, and will make its conclusions known to the providers by giving or withholding its support and patronage. At the moment, wholly subsidised leisure provision is regarded by most taxpayers (especially local taxpayers) as an extravagance. However this may be, it is true that an increase in competition is usually of benefit to the consumer, and this was certainly true in the leisure industry where outdated and badly maintained facilities were expensive loss makers, because they lay ignored and unused while customers frequented well-marketed private sector provision.

In the past, it has been too often forgotten that looking after clients must mean regular physical improvement and refurbishment of buildings and playing areas. It is commonsense that public buildings should be made accessible and user friendly, but the public also demand a safe and pleasant ambience so security and cleanliness are important selling points.

This explains why, in the last three or four years, we have seen improvements in the quality of facilities offered to a more discerning public. After all, no commercial venue which had frayed carpets, torn seats, dirty, neglected approaches and surly staff would survive very long, and now they no longer have a monopoly local authorities are turning their minds to marketing strategies.

Offering a service

What, then, is marketing? In the world of leisure provision, we are not offering a commodity like a loaf of bread, a washing powder or a motor car. We are offering a service. Sometimes we are selling the right to use facilities for a given period of time, as in a squash court, a fitness suite or a swimming pool; sometimes we are selling seats in a theatre or hall and supplying musicians, actors, dancers or other entertainers. The commercial sector is adept at providing services of competitive quality because, by their very nature, they are immediately accountable if custom falls away. Hotels, restaurants, private golf or health clubs and holiday villages have long known that the customer must perceive that he or she is getting value for money. Such organisations monitor the pricing policies, quality standards and market success of their competitors very carefully, and jealously guard their niche in the market. Now that subsidies are dwindling, the public sectors are going to have to look closely at the environment in which their services are provided – at, for instance, location, style furnishings, colour, layout and noise levels.

In an outspoken and challenging article in *The Leisure Manager* (January 1991) entitled 'Can leisure survive the public sector?', Christopher Guest, Marketing Officer for Sandwell Metropolitan Borough Council Department of Leisure, has this to say:

> Every time a customer walks through the doors of a leisure facility the whole local authority is on trial: from the cleanliness of the building, the interaction and treatment by staff and the overall quality of the range of services on offer. In other words, any local authority ought to strive for the pursuit of excellence. If local government is to have a future then it has to search for alternative management philosophies to enable it to survive … the Chartered Institute of Marketing's own definition of marketing in the public sector is: 'The management process responsible for identifying, anticipating and satisfying customer requirements cost effectively'. What better ideals should we embrace to ensure that leisure survives the public sector?

Put simply, since customers are the ones who exercise choice in the market place, marketing is the art of making it easier for the customer to say 'yes'.

It will be appreciated that marketing is not to be viewed just as selling, just as advertising or any other such single element, but as a complete philosophy. It is an art – the art of running and managing a business, a facility, a complex or a service department, so that customers are happy because they feel that they are getting what they paid for. Over the course of time, it is also important that they should feel that the 'product' is consistent in quality, and so will keep coming back for more. All successful service is a matter of pleasing people – and good managers realise this. On the wall of its service department one motor company main dealer has a notice: 'If we don't look after our customers somebody else will', which is a concise way of emphasising that it is by the customers' direct experience of a service that the whole organisation will stand or fall … and that implies more than a synthetic smile and a stereotyped 'Have a nice day!'

Liz Terry, the editor of *Leisure Management*, makes a heartfelt plea for greater sincerity, and a higher standard of customer care:

> 'Service with a Smile'. 'The Customer is King'. 'The Customer Counts' … All great platitudes [obvious remarks] of the British service industries. Platitudes because we say these things without actually believing them, and because they have lost their true meaning for those who are responsible for putting the philosophy into practice: staff. The British have a long history of excellence in the service industries. The English butler is seen as having achieved the ultimate in terms of service delivery; English bar staff

have invented some of the finest cocktails, and British shopkeepers gave a name to the nation.

Despite these traditions and examples of British service at its best, we seem to have lost the art, and the leisure industry is in dire need of a reaffirmation of the importance of good customer care. . . Training staff to bleat monotonous greetings is an entirely superficial and cosmetic exercise. The real point to customer care is to create a service which speaks for itself in terms of excellence, attention to detail and customer needs, and then to enhance it with attention from staff who have been trained to treat customers with warmth and a personal touch. This is a tall order, and not something which can happen overnight, but it is important that the industry adopts professional personnel methods in its approach to customer care and customer care training, and that attention is paid to the real issue, which is the fact that the initial service must be superb; fast, and, accurate, with attention to detail and fulfilling every promise made in its marketing: the final effect is made by staff in the delivery of the service. Coin a welcome greeting, but let it be seen as just that, something unique to your operation, something appropriate to your organisation and train your staff in the skills necessary to allow them to use this as part of their own approach to customers.

Train them in crisis management, in cash control, in organisation. Teach them how to keep difficult customers under control, how to do their jobs so efficiently that they will have some energy left for customers.

Customer surveys

Giving the customers what they want might sound simple, but it is not always easy to find what will get people out of their homes, for the lure of the television set, the satisfactions of DIY activities, and other home-based hobbies, can be powerful incentives to stay indoors. We pointed out earlier that the backgrounds and work situations of potential clients must be studied carefully, and to identify customers more exactly we can initiate market research and customer-attitude surveys. Above all, customer complaints are valuable marketing aids, for by listening to what clients do not like or even feel resentful about, staff will be able to react positively to what the public needs. Because one dissatisfied person can put off dozens of potential customers just by airing his or her views, a good 'press' and enthusiastic word-of-mouth recommendations from satisfied users are essential to the success of any venture, however big or small, and customer orientated leisure centres would be wise to display in their foyers that favourite sign found in hairdressers, big stores, and the like: 'If we have pleased you, tell others; if not, tell us.'

As well as taking note of customer reaction it is an essential practical step to obtain the names and addresses of as many visitors as possible, so that a mailing list may be built up. Questionnaires are a simple and useful way of gathering information, but most people are busy and a complex set of questions which require long written answers can be counter productive, for they will be brushed aside or rushed through, and can easily irritate potential customers. The art of composing a good questionnaire is to formulate a set of short questions which require either a tick in a box or a simple yes/no answer.

It is essential to read the reports of surveys conducted by specialists, such as Mintel, Gallup and the Policy Studies Institute, excerpts from which are frequently printed in newspapers or trade journals. These are especially useful because they reflect views and trends over a wide spectrum of society and so provide valuable statistics for government planners and business operators. Conferences, forums, seminars and other forms of information sharing help to generate enthusiasm among organisers of provision and their staff at the same time that they help to explore customers' needs. The whole secret of successful marketing is to put oneself in the customer's place and see the product or service through his or her eyes.

Now that many centres combine entertainments with sport and physical activities, directors have had to investigate the varied musical tastes of individuals from the widest cross-section of their catchment area, and as there are so many people of different ages and interests, a well-balanced music programme would have to offer pop, rock, folk, jazz, classical, country, blues, etc., so that everyone might be catered for.

Stage entertainments must also be varied and broadly based. Managers would hope to see performances ranging from children's shows and comedians to performances by local operatic and dramatic societies, as well as visiting professional theatre companies and one-man shows. The important point is that the facilities should be kept in use for 52 weeks a year, because if the people are coming in, it does not matter if there is a film society showing in progress or a trade exhibition being staged, as long as the building is bustling: busy premises are a sign of a commercial success story.

Leisure consultants

At the beginning of this chapter we noted that local authorities are advertising for commercial partners, and so perhaps now we should dwell briefly on the type of service offered by leisure consultants and ask what they do. They:

- give invaluable advice on the choice of location for new facilities;
- obtain information on transport networks;
- provide a full social and cultural survey of an area.

Naturally, they are well acquainted with the latest leisure trends and fashions, and have contacts to provide everything from croquet lawns to Karaoke evenings, if required. Some of them will even establish staff and management training programmes to help with the all-important training in customer care. They are the marketing experts, but it does help if all of us, as students of leisure provision, have some knowledge of and practice in the skills and techniques by which they earn their fees. Examples of leisure consultants' claims might make clear the extent of the planning and marketing problems that are arising in the industry:

1. Our Management Consulting Team understands CCT. More importantly, we know how it can stretch your time and resources to the limit. We can complement your own skills with sensitive, practical and independent advice. Currently, we are advising metropolitan boroughs, district councils and other public sector organisations.

****

2. Are you developing or operating golf or leisure facilities?

Are your calculations correct?
Have you considered the full potential?
Are you using the best range of facilities?
Is your marketing plan fully developed?
How are the facilities to be operated?
Is your development budget on target?
Is your design satisfactory?

We can provide detailed feasibility studies.
We can prepare full financial appraisals.
We can arrange comprehensive marketing reports.
We can design an optimum range of facilities.
We can prepare detailed operational structures.
We can troubleshoot existing centres.
We can provide a full development package.

****

THE MUSEUM CONSULTANCY SERVICE
Professional consultancy for museums from museum
professionals:
Exhibit plans, corporate plans, business plans,
development plans, extension plans, feasibility programmes,
revenue generation programmes, space and facility
programmes,
collection development strategies
The Museum Consultancy Service has the expertise to provide
the solutions to your problems.

These examples give some idea of the help that strategic consultancy expertise can offer to both public and private clients, and it is said that though the private sector client is more businesslike and has clearer objectives than the public counterpart, clients' awareness of the consultancy role in the latter sector is improving.

The four Ps

We see then, that marketing requires research of customer wants, analysis and then provision of the service or product. Marketing men talk about 'the four Ps': delivering the right *Product* (or service) at the right *Place* and the right *Price*, and, finally, ensuring that it is effectively *Promoted*.

Analysing a product (or service) is essential for effective marketing, and a SWOT (Strengths, Weaknesses, Opportunities and Threats) analysis is often used; for example, a SWOT analysis of local authority leisure services might be something like this:

Strengths: reasonably priced, often free, promotes health, quality of life, includes the disadvantaged, linked to tourism, dedicated and committed staff, control of land, multi-purpose building, joint use of local authority facilities.

Weaknesses: outdoor facilities dependent on weather, not enough indoor provision, often poor locations, facilities in need of renewal, refurbishment or replacement, too much emphasis on young, councillors often unrepresentative and out of touch with current thinking.

Opportunities: expanding market, increase in standards of living, more leisure time, concern for fitness, subsidies.

Threats: central government legislation, reduction of financial support, increased competition from private sector.

After analysing the *product* by means of the SWOT technique, it is necessary to look at the other three 'Ps' to see what improvements and developments may be made in customer service.

Place. Unfavourable location of premises could be helped by organising a tie up with public transport authorities for the advantage of both parties. Mobile schemes for taking the service to the people – a playbus, action sport teams, outreach, a mobile library fleet, for example, – might be considered. Mobile fitness-testing teams could be set up to visit venues in outlying areas. Centralising very specialist activities, for example, ski-slopes, ice skating and dancing, cross-country loops, and climbing walls, at particular locations. Engage a team of experts to teach canoeing, scuba-diving and synchronised swimming at under-used conventional swimming pools. Establish in-house crèches and carefully plan sessions for sport and activities to help deliver services at the right place and time.

Price. Special tickets for different age groups, special tickets for unemployed and disadvantaged users, books of tickets, discounts, off-peak pricing, use of 'loss-leader' and free-trial tickets.

Promotion. Video/slide presentations and talks in schools, community centres, clubs; video-wall advertising in shopping centres, community centres; exhibitions in libraries, museums, tourist information offices; advertising in local press plus local radio and television; advertising notices in all local authority buildings, on local transport and in offices.

The over fifties market

Every product, however good, has, after its introduction, periods of growth, maturity and decline. The task facing the marketing minded provider of leisure facilities when the appeal of a service or attraction begins to diminish is to find new markets and introduce new ideas. Let us look, for instance, at a newly identified market: leisure for the over 50s. Older consumers have, in the past, been neglected by the leisure industry, so, if the market for youngsters participating in sports, going to the cinema or using nightclubs is diminishing, why not, as there is a fall in the number of 15–24 year-olds, focus attention on the growth in the number of people over 50 years of age?

To the older generation, 'leisure' is perhaps an alien concept, because many of the activities which are common today were unavailable to them or beyond their means. They may be uneasy about fun and freedom of activity, thinking 'This is not our thing'. Such attitudes are a barrier to participation. Older consumers are as varied in their expectations and wealth as any other age group, so we should be working as much towards the abolition of ageism as towards the abolition of sexism and racism. People over 50 must be helped to become 'leisure literate', that is, to appreciate the opportunities on offer and to exploit those opportunties to full advantage, thus improving their quality of life.

The report, *What's Age Got to do With It?* ('Leisure for the over 50s – An Unfulfilled Market', Leisure Marketplace, Abingdon, Oxon.) targets an affluent group with a disposable income of £108 billion, which already spends 13 per cent more than the national average on holidays, cars and durables. We have noted that occupational pension schemes are improving rapidly, but we do not always remember that an increasing number of working women have pensions in their own right, nor that growth in home ownership means that retired people have usually accumulated substantial capital wealth when mortgages have been paid off and family obligations have been fulfilled.

The loss of the work role due to earlier retirement can mean that the social interaction formerly enjoyed in the workplace has to be replaced in retirement, and this is where the active use of leisure time to provide intellectual and physical stimulation becomes socially important, as well as offering an untapped leisure market. There should, therefore, be a balance between commercial opportunities and social needs.

New attraction ideas

As well as targeting neglected groups of consumers, those who market leisure are turning their minds to new ideas, and, though many themes have been borrowed from the USA, some are home-grown. For example, Chessington World of Adventure has recently invested £8 million in building a Transylvanian-style village complete with Dracula's castle and a terrifying Vampire Ride, which takes clients on a hanging rollercoaster above the trees and below the ground; this development is helping to boost attendances to over two million per annum.

Remote and old-fashioned country hotels have enjoyed increased trade by arranging 'murder weekends' during which guests become part of an Agatha Christie style mystery, where a crime is committed and they themselves become actors and participants. For the conservation minded holiday-maker, Holiday Club Pontins is offering a series of Nature Conservation Weekends at Barton Hall, a Victorian mansion near Torquay. Guests are offered animal tracking, badger watches and late-night bat hunts, all using the latest methods of electronic surveillance.

In an effort to attract trade and generate revenue, period themes

The Ironbridge Gorge Museum's Blists Hill site. An industrial township of one hundred years ago has been re-created around the working remains of the Industrial Revolution and is a major tourist attraction.

(Photograph courtesy of Ironbridge Museum Trust.)

by which the customer imagines he or she is transported in time as well as space are also becoming popular. Bournemouth, for example, has an annual 'Forties Festival' which includes a 40s fashion show, 40s-style dancing, vintage coach tours and 40s music recitals. This mixture of nostalgia and history is made more authentic by a 'war and peace' theme, which includes an air show over the seafront and outings to the former homes of Lord Mountbatten and other prominent historical figures.

The city of Bradford in West Yorkshire has for some time now been pursuing an innovative and aggressive marketing campaign capitalising on its own past, as well as nearby tourist attractions such as the Brontë Country and the village which is the fictional Beckingdale of Yorkshire Television's *Emmerdale*. In the city itself, attractions as diverse as the National Museum of Photography, Film and Television, the birthplace of Delius and the Sooty Museum have been developed. A 'Flavours of Asia' holiday break is successfully marketed featuring the food, faiths and festivals of Bradford's Asian community. As a result of these and other interesting ventures, five million people (including 250,000 foreign tourists) visit the area each year, contributing £5 million to the local economy: so, the image of Bradford has been improved, business has been generated, the number of jobs has increased, there is a new local pride and tourism seems assured of a future. The lesson to be learned from Bradford is that every area has some historical or cultural connection which will enrich the leisure of others and which is a potential income earner if research and planning are properly carried out.

Earlier, we looked briefly at the dockland developments of Cardiff and Liverpool, but it must be remembered that these are merely two very well-known, large-scale developments. All over the British Isles, disused industrial buildings in ugly surroundings are being given a new image by architects, made viable by a mix of specialist retail, entertainment, food and drink venues, and then by skilful marketing, are being promoted as lively places to live, work and play. This movement from dereliction to development is one of the most encouraging trends of the 1990s, and it is likely to continue as long as all sectors of the leisure industry co-operate to think creatively and market their assets profitably.

The improvement and exploitation of natural resources is occupying the minds of leisure developers at the moment, but this is a very sensitive area, since in a small country like ours wild and unspoilt environments are themselves rare and valuable. Most people, for example, do not object to the substitution of a marina and leisure centre for a disused commercial dock, but attempts to exploit and commercialise rivers or even rural canals can meet with strong resistance. The approach to marketing any new leisure facility should be a sympathetic and tactful one, and must take into account the density of the existing population. There may be little opposition to another environmentally friendly Scottish ski resort in the remote Highlands near Fort William, which is genuinely needed to spread the increasing demand at the other four centres in Scotland, but developers may find difficulties in establishing the need for yet another waterpark, theme park or shopping/leisure complex in the crowded south east of England.

Successful marketing can often be much cheaper and simpler than in some of the large-scale projects outlined above, and good practice along with some bright ideas can attract publicity and new users. Several leisure centres, for example, finding that they had under-used indoor space, have established all-weather 'projectile halls' for use in such sports as archery, rifle/pistol shooting, golf driving and so on. The capital expense of such adaptation is minimal and re-conversion is easily possible if tastes and demands change again.

Catching the public's imagination

Ideas which catch the public's imagination, such as the interactive 'Launch Pad' displays at London's Science Museum, attract custom from whole families, generate income and fulfil an educational purpose. When children's curiosity and meddlesome instincts were kept in check by an army of attendants, 'glass-case paranoia' meant that children were hostile to the atmosphere of museums; now over

The Albert Dock, Liverpool. This once derelict dockland site has been turned into a thriving community of shops, restaurants, public houses, wine bars, galleries and museums.

800,000 visit the Science Museum each year, and other museums are realising that as there are 32,000 primary schools in Britain, there is a vast market for hands-on exhibits. Teachers who have scrutinised the educational claims of such displays have agreed that the changes in the museum world do have relevance to the National Curriculum. It is said that the vital ingredients of good interactive exhibits are that they contain a thought-provoking element of surprise, combined with a satisfying sense of being in control. Education through entertainment is a worthwhile objective for any branch of the leisure industry, and the success of some modern museums illustrates the constant need to appraise and invest in a product or service if it is to retain its position and reputation.

Sometimes good marketing practice can consist simply of making the reception area of a facility more welcoming. It is surprising to note how many centres which have expensive equipment and well-trained staff still have a reception area which is full of barriers to communication that confuse rather than clarify. For first-time visitors especially, clear way marking and effective, attractive signage is essential, so those who are in charge of leisure facilities must acquire or develop some knowledge of display skills. Something as obvious as a redesigned uniform can change the image of a facility by helping to create a relaxed atmosphere and present a friendlier image to the public. A more open style of management will also encourage a happier work atmosphere, and if senior management could be required to work periodically alongside staff, they would demonstrate their commitment to the values which they preach. A feeling of identity is created when employees believe that they have a recognisable role to play within an organisation, and if their suggestions are valued by management they will enjoy increased job satisfaction and perform better, benefiting themselves, the customer and the organisation.

Company policy, especially in the 'enjoyment business', is likely to be more successful when it concentrates on operational flexibility and employee participation, rather than establishing outmoded dictatorial hierarchies. After all, our Japanese competitors in the motor industry taught us that organisations should aim to create an ethos which inspires staff loyalty, not least because a shared vision among staff leads to a healthy and profitable operation.

As cleanliness, safety and environmental protection are now so prominent in the minds of the public, all who work in the leisure industry should be well informed about technical developments and new equipment; a high-profile, caring image is essential if clients are to feel that they are spending their money in the pursuit of enjoyment that will not harm themselves or anyone else. Consumer research has revealed that one reason for the success of the transport systems known as people carriers is that they make people feel cared for and protected, while from the point of view of the management of zoos, leisure parks and shopping centres these automatic guided vehicles (AGVs) have no rails, are pollution-free and easy to install; also, because like monorail cars they are computer guided, they need no staff to operate them.

Technical developments

Of course, as well as making friends, safe and efficient operation maximises profits, so it is essential for the educated leisure employee to have some knowledge of the ways in which today's technology can help business. We mentioned earlier the advantages of installing heat-exchangers between warm-water pools and ice pads, but in the interests of minimising heat loss and evaporation, we need to know about pool covers and solar heaters. Equipment for waterplay and play equipment for children is constantly being made safer and more attractive, so that the relative cost, appeal and durability of rival systems will have to be evaluated.

No new idea, sport or product which relates to leisure can be ignored. Consider orienteering which has grown rapidly in popularity because it is a green, safe form of exercise, which rocketed in popularity after being dubbed 'the natural sport for the thinking runner'! Consider how in tune with today's thinking is the laser system of clay pigeon shooting which is good sport but makes no noise, burns no powder and targets re-usable clays. Similarly, paintball and laser shooting games have met with great success from operators and customers alike, so that today these games are European competitor sports with a major market in the corporate entertainment and hospitality sector.

New safety surfaces for indoor and outdoor use are constantly being developed, and much reading will be necessary to ensure that one is familiar with innovations in this all-important branch of leisure technology. Even the study of surface-cleaning machinery is vital if we are to attract the discriminating customer of the contemporary leisure market.

It is not enough simply to read the brochures or take the word of the purveyors of advanced equipment, because the public needs the unbiased, independent, guidance that must come from the leisure expert, not the commercial salesman. Most people, for example, would like a smooth, even suntan, but since scientific research has revealed that harmful wavelengths in both infra-red and ultraviolet light may cause premature ageing of the skin or even cancer, popularity of sunbeds has waned, and until new products are shown to be beneficial there is likely to be a drop in market demand that can only be reversed by knowledge and sensitivity. It has also been found that some strength developing machines and aerobic exercisers can lead to physical injuries. Thus, as long as the fashion for bronzed skin and the demand for cardiovascular exercise fitness systems continue, the leisure professional will have to know the difference between machinery which is health enhancing, and that which is positively harmful. This means that in order to develop and sustain business in the health market we shall have to investigate the claims of manufacturers.

Automation can be a great boon to the operators of public houses, late-night stores, wine bars, sandwich bars as well as theme parks, and leisure centres. In the bad old days, the lack of catering in 'out of hours' periods was said to be because staff were unwilling to work late shifts and unsocial hours. Machines have no such reservations and dispense refreshment on a round-the-clock basis with absolute consistency of service. The state-of-the-art vending machines of today offer much more than cans of drink and coffee in a plastic cup. Chips, deep-fried in oil, can be ready within 60 seconds accompanied by salt, vinegar, ketchup or mayonnaise as required. There are even fully automatic restaurants which can vend anything from a main course served on a nine-inch china plate, to fruit, yoghurt or cheese and biscuits! Such machines are controlled by a microprocessor, which also diagnoses any faults and operates an automatic health timer to check the temperature of food.

Apart from automated outlets, fast-food catering has proved that it is here to stay and is very profitable. Bowling centres conducted market research and found that having a hamburger and a drink were regarded as being part of the bowling experience, and well-designed, high-quality snack bars undoubtedly helped in attracting a more affluent, family-orientated outlet. Most sectors of the leisure industry have already recognised the importance of promoting catering as an integral part of their operations, and regard eating as a leisure activity, employing special marketing tactics designed to keep children happy. The expanding leisure market is becoming more competitive, and operators must upgrade their facilities and add new services and profit centres to their core businesses.

It has often been said that fashions and novelties come and go, but people still have to eat and it makes sense to market good, value-for-money catering. If a venue has good food and beverage (F & B) outlets conveniently placed near to attractions, there is nothing wrong in indulging in a little light-hearted marketing. Thus at The Dome near Doncaster, one can have a Splash N' Hash breakfast and a Dip N' Chips lunch by the pool, while users of the ice pads can have a Skate N' Flakes breakfast and a Ice N' Slice lunch! After all, it does not take a medical expert to work out that when people exercise, they generally become hungry.

Revamping old ideas

Any new market is worthy of attention, and in marketing the philosophy is not to look at successful innovations with envy but to imitate them. Also, if an old idea which was once popular has become dated and neglected, the sensible thing to do is to recover its former appeal by reviewing technology for new variations on the old theme. A good example of this is thalasso therapy. The term comes from the Greek word 'thalassa', or sea water, and it is the prevention or treatment of physical and neurological disorders using the sea's muds, weeds, sands, water and climate. What else is that but the same formula which caused Brighton to boom in the nineteenth century and led to the popularity of brine baths and mud baths right up to the Second World War? The sea's healing properties have long been recognised, but such treatment became unfashionable 50 years ago. Now revamped and based on wet cures (whirlpool baths, multi-jet baths, algae therapy, high power showers, underwater showers and jet streams) and dry cures (massage, exercise, saunas, infra-red light, electrical cures, sand or sea mud baths), techniques which have been known in Britain for two centuries have become fashionable in France where 21 thalasso centres are worth more than £35 million to the French leisure industry. Many people taking thalasso treatments are ill or convalescing, but some enjoy taking treatments in their leisure time, for relaxation and recuperation. The popularity of the old health hydros and spas in general confirms an existing link between medicine and leisure which might be profitably revived in Britain, especially in view of the rise in the market for the over 50s which we noted earlier. Such a revival might have a beneficial environmental effect on the waters around the British coast, for, if clean, unpolluted sea water were to become a money spinner, many seaside authorities would quickly improve the quality of their water.

Of course, too much gimmickry can make consumers think the leisure operator is jumping on a bandwagon, and can mean the spending of huge sums to create attractions that might slump in popularity before they have recouped their capital outlay. We have already warned that we must not make the mistakes of disfiguring the natural environment. At the same time, we can observe the large number of successful heritage centres and theme parks busy re-creating the past or simulating the future. If consumers sometimes question the integrity of centres which use the techniques of set building, prop making, figure sculpting, scenic painting, glass fibre moulding and sound and light systems, all of which seem to have more to do with film and television than with history, operators are quick to point to their growing receipts and to quote the example of Disney's phenomenal multi-national triumphs, which are based on exactly the same formula. It is difficult to know where to draw the line sometimes. How, for instance, does one judge an underground interpretive display in a mining reconstruction at the Black Country Museum in the West Midlands, where sound effects create the creaking of pit-props, light and sound together imitate controlled blasting with falling coal noises, and there is even a section of floor powered by hydraulic rams to make the ground vibrate underfoot? Is all that drama justifiable if one is attempting to give a total impression of what the life of a miner was like? Certainly, it creates an experience, and after all, one could hardly subject visitors and school parties to the real thing! The matter of what is valid interpretive art and what is sensationalist fantasy must be left to the taste and discretion of directors and consultants. It is interesting to learn that one heritage consultancy has coined the slogan: 'The past has a big future!'

The European perspective

Whatever else we may think, we must decide to look at marketing and provision from a European perspective. The combined effect of the single European market, deregulated air fairs and the Channel Tunnel may be seen either as a threat to the British tourist and leisure industry or a significant opportunity. For one thing, Europe, because of different retirement and pension arrangements, has more active and prosperous 'third agers' than this country. (Third agers are those who have gone through the age of learning, the age of working and are now in the age of living.) European and American families expect a more welcoming attitude to children in food outlets, accommodation and attractions. So it would appear that we shall have to do some thinking about targeting age and interest groups if we are to maintain a leading edge in leisure.

One challenge which comes along with an influx of cosmopolitan visitors is that they often bring with them higher expectations of facilities and service, so that a major need created by the Channel Tunnel will be an improvement in our existing leisure and tourism product, and that, in turn, will mean increased availability of well-trained and motivated multi-lingual staff.

An example of good marketing practice

Before concluding this chapter, it would be as well to look at an example of good marketing practice, which will serve to remind us that selling leisure is not like selling soap, and that in the quest to promote our product and remain viable, we must not lose sight of wider issues such as the refreshment of mind and spirit and the need for social values.

The Countryside Commission, in addition to being the official adviser to the government on countryside matters, has responsibility for the 10 National Parks which cover 10 per cent of the land area of England and Wales. The 75 per cent of their net costs for the National Parks paid by central government (in 1991–2) is a relatively small total of £22.6 million. Though the Commission estimates that three-quarters of the population visits the countryside each year, spending £12.5 billion and supporting as many jobs as agriculture, more visitors and income are still necessary for the costly job of countryside management. In consequence, a campaign has been launched to increase public awareness of the nation's beauty spots, encourage a greater interest in the environment, improve the standard of facilities offered at country parks and persuade ethnic minority groups to enjoy the countryside.

The Commission is to introduce a beauty spots rating plan – a sort of Egon Ronay-style check in the quality of service offered in rural areas as well as providing information about access and features of interest. In order to encourage ethnic minority groups from the inner cities to venture beyond the urban landscape, the Commission is publishing promotional material in ethnic languages and including black or Asian faces in printed publicity alongside the 'usual smiling, white middle-class couples'. The practical step has also been taken of setting a target of 2 per cent of people who are employed in such jobs as wardens, rangers or builders of stone walls being drawn from ethnic minority groups, in order to make members of such groups feel welcome in the countryside. Thus, commonsense, sensitivity and innovation will be combined to increase social awareness while opening up another market, channel profits from tourism into countryside conservation and promote a splendid sector of the British heritage – effective marketing with foresight and integrity.

However skilful marketing personnel may be, their efforts will be wasted unless leisure centres, museums, theatres and other providers have the right staff to ensure the organisation's success. In the next chapter we shall examine the leisure industry's greatest asset, the human resources of skill, sincerity and dedication it can draw upon.

7   Who gets the job?

We have looked at the boom in leisure and seen how provision has improved over the course of more than a century of leisure evolution. We have looked at those who consume leisure services and those who supply them, at the way in which money is found to pay for this provision and at how leisure provision is marketed. What we have not considered so far is who actually undertakes the day-to-day running of leisure services, makes them available and provides help and guidance to the public.

Customer care

However we choose to spend our leisure time (and our money), we always look for enjoyment and like to feel that our lives have been enriched by our experiences. It is the quality of people whom we encounter at the 'interface' – that point where staff and public meet – which is usually the most important factor in determining the extent of our satisfaction. Often, when the exact surroundings and precise sensations of our holidays and outings have become blurred by time and all but forgotten, we still remember the personnel we came into contact with. We recall with pleasure those who were friendly and had time to talk to us as individuals. We respect and, perhaps, envy the professional skills and knowledge of coaches, instructors, guides and organisers, but most of all we value their patience, kindness and humour as they help us to learn, improve and enjoy an activity. Even brief contact with staff who operate transport systems or run ticket offices can make an impression which affects for better or worse our appreciation of the whole experience. Courtesy, cheerfulness and efficiency will create happy memories which will bring us back to a venue again and again. Rudeness, carelessness and incompetence will drive us away. We may stay away and also tell others about our disappointment. Staff can be an organisation's greatest asset, or its worst liability. So the answer to our question, 'Who gets the job?', must be: those individuals who are competent, confident and who, above all, have interpersonal skills and a genuine vocation for 'the people business', which means regarding the happiness of others as being at least as important as their own. Employers are very well aware that the quality of their service is, in the last analysis, in the hands of their staff, and for this reason it will be useful for us to examine a selection of advertisements for staff vacancies. As we have seen, there are many aspects to the world of leisure, and it would be impossible to cover all the different types of jobs offered at all levels within the public, private and voluntary sectors. Because so many posts are widely advertised in the press for local authority employees, and because those vacancies are often more carefully defined than in the private sector, we are going to concentrate more on the skills and qualities demanded by leisure providers in the public sector.

As so many of us get our most frequent experiences of contact with leisure professionals at leisure centres, let us look first at the range of jobs offered in this field. Leisure attendants, or leisure assistants, can be full-time or part-time. These all-important jobs are the ones with most customer contact, they are usually hourly-paid and are often the first step on the ladder for those who wish to make a career in a leisure environment. The work of such an attendant is generally described as something like this:

> 'Main duties: supervision of centre users, assembling and dismantling sports equipment, maintaining cleanliness and hygiene within the centre; some poolside duties.'

Some points are worth noting. First, 'cleanliness and hygiene within the centre' can mean, among other things, cleaning the lavatories. When asked about this, the area manager of a large complex of facilities said that he always makes this point clear when drafting advertisements because many applicants with academic qualifications expect to come straight into an administrative post when beginning their careers, and might not realise that some grandiose phrase such as, 'control and organisation of facilities to ensure a safe recreational environment' means in practice, 'swabbing out changing-rooms and toilet areas'! Second, the same manager made it clear that he would not offer a post to any attendant who did not possess the Royal Life Saving Society (RLSS) Bronze Award, arguing that as rota systems are worked in most centres, each attendant will regularly be on 'wet' duties as well as 'dry' ones. Some employers are willing to take on leisure assistants without the RLSS Bronze, but only on condition that they gain the award within three or four months of starting the job. Third, shift working is essential for, as the manager pointed out, centres open at 7 am and commonly close at 11 pm – often later if the function rooms are in use. Also, employees will sometimes have to work during weekends and public holidays. When asked if he tried to recruit individuals with marked sporting abilities, the manager said that was not always a good idea, as most sports and games in Britain are played at weekends, which is the time when centres are at their busiest, so that employing exceptional sportspeople often led to a conflict of interests.

Equal opportunities

When advertising posts, some employers declare their equal opportunities policy clearly: 'We positively encourage applications from black people, and those from other ethnic minorities, people with disabilities and women where they are under-represented in the workforce.' Of course, this excellent policy cannot always be implemented for all jobs, and for obvious reasons, separate advertisements have to be devised for male and female changing-room attendants. Similarly, all pool attendants have, of necessity, to be able-bodied. Yet, as the leisure centre manager pointed out, people with disabilities can and do work in the offices of several of the facilities under his control. Birmingham City Council has an even more explicit policy on the equality issue stating: 'The City Council welcomes applications from all sections of the community, irrespective of race, colour, gender, sexuality or disability. Job sharers welcome, no partner necessary.' In a caring industry like the leisure industry, sensitivity to the needs of minority groups is essential and would-be employees must appreciate this in advance of any application, so many authorities specifically state: 'Understanding of equal opportunities is a key to this post', or 'A commitment to the practice of equal opportunities is essential', and sometimes, 'Contacts with local black and Asian communities would be an advantage', and, for some jobs 'It would be of benefit to have worked directly with ethnic groups in the community'. In an effort to ensure that minorities take advantage of the facilities offered within the district, some councils advertise for Asian sportsworkers, 'Because we are taking a new innovative approach to encourage members of the Asian Community to take part in sports and recreation, applicant must be able to speak Hindi, Urdu or Punjabi.'

Personal qualities

Office and catering jobs in leisure departments can be very rewarding – always as long as applicants realise that, unlike some other businesses, there is no question of a nine to five day, and that they have been warned that, 'This post will involve working unsocial hours'. The result is that ticket clerks, receptionists, cafeteria and bar staff have a pattern of shift working, just as the leisure assistants and managerial staffs have.

The qualities demanded by employers for their leisure attendants and assistants seem to be much the same throughout the country. The phrase 'Enthusiasm, energy and commitment' appears again and again in advertisements, as does 'Ability to deal with the public at all levels, exhibiting confidence and good communication skills.' Some authorities make a point of saying that they are seeking staff with a 'Respectful but firm attitude with members of the public.' Others more ambitiously ask for 'Initiative, versatility, responsibility. Must be energetic, physically fit and able to supervise others.' Many specify that those appointed will be 'Hardworking and conscientious, with an outgoing personality.' All, it appears, want someone who is 'Courteous, with a friendly and helpful manner who is genuinely interested in providing a service.' The sincerity and integrity of the employee is very much valued, and some advertisements pointedly inform applicants that they 'Must enjoy working with the public – especially children', while one centre advises that they 'Must have a flair for customer care'!

Clerical assistants and receptionists are front-line ambassadors for any swimming-pool complex, sports hall or entertainment venue, and advertisements for such posts usually demand that 'Applicants should have good communication and interpersonal skills geared towards a successful customer care policy.' A senior ticket clerk at a leisure centre is expected to undertake reception and cashier duties, supervise the ticket office, prepare monthly accounts and tabulate usage figures. The qualifications needed for the post include 'Experience in running a busy office and must be capable of operating a full booking system, membership scheme, have an aptitude for figures and be capable of dealing with a computerized booking system.' Applicants for most clerical jobs are required to 'Have the ability to deal with the general public in a very busy environment', as well as 'A sound educational background with emphasis on written English and numeracy skills.' Some employers are more precise about academic standards and ask for 'A minimum of three GCSE passes (A, B or C) or equivalent.' An essential requirement seems to be 'Smart appearance, pleasant manner and an aptitude for dealing with customers.' Some advertisements just state 'Should be able to demonstrate the right personality', and leave applicants to work out what that should be. Presumably that would equate with the need for a candidate who should be 'Friendly, helpful, flexible in approach and able to work as a member of a team. Must have GCSE (or equivalent) English, plus typing and keyboard skills.' Some advertisers add thoughtfully 'Must be able to work with a wide range of people, including those with disabilities, in a sensitive manner.' Another leisure centre manager advertises honestly and clearly for 'A tireless assistant able to clear paperwork, radiate enthusiasm and keep the office running smoothly' – a very realistic approach!

There are also good employment opportunities for specialist sports practitioners, and high annual salaries are offered. You might see advertisements for a coaching/course co-ordinator ('To assist in the administration, marketing and provision of coaching courses'), or for a swimming lesson co-ordinator ('To co-ordinate the schools' lessons programme and the popular private lessons' scheme. Some teaching involved and organisation of others on the scheme').

The coaching job stipulates 'A desire to help handicapped and elderly people', along with 'Coaching qualifications and the ability to teach a number of sports.' The swimming co-ordinator is required to be 'A good organiser and qualified to a minimum of Amateur Swimming Association (ASA) or the Swimming Teachers' Association (STA) advanced award.'

Recently demand has arisen for fitness instructors, and there are good opportunities for those who 'Have had some experience in the operation of weight resistant and cardiovascular equipment and some knowledge of fitness testing.' Perhaps very wisely, the proviso has been added 'First-aid qualifications are desirable'. Additionally, there is a need for a 'Fitness Consultant to manage a club-style health and fitness studio which includes 19 of the most up-to-date fitness stations, sauna, steam room and jacuzzi. Must be able to take complete responsibility from introductory sessions to organising general fitness programmes.'

Some authorities look to the future, realising that they must train potential managers in order that the service can have continuity and consistency; so there are excellent opportunities for able people with enthusiasm, energy and a commitment to the leisure industry to become trainee leisure managers and 'Develop knowledge and experience in all aspects of the business from leisure administration to marketing, sponsorship and special events. Applicants may hold or be studying towards a leisure-based qualification.' Similarly, some district councils advertise for graduate trainees and ask for submissions from 'Persons of graduate calibre for training over a wide area of Leisure and Amenity Services to enable the postholder to develop a career through professional examinations.'

In-service training

Great emphasis is placed on in-service training as well as formal courses of study. John Trower, the manager of leisure services in

South Shropshire spoke frankly about the need for continuous, effective staff training:

> We did in-house training pretty amateurishly for a while, I suppose, but we are now going through a detailed analysis of quality provision, and as part of that the staff are being told to do things in certain ways, down to answering the telephone and anticipating customer requirements and the uniform that is worn. All staff (including part-timers) receive detailed training embracing things such as filling in accident forms, completing reports and, of course, familiarity with health and safety regulations, so that the people who work here understand issues relating to the operation of centres – right down to the nuts and bolts of day-to-day running.

He also mentioned how thorough the methods of making appointments had to be nowadays:

> We spend a lot of time even at leisure assistant level to make sure that we get the right people, and after that they go through a probationary period to check that they are conforming to our pattern. We have intensive group discussions, we have aptitude tests, intelligence tests, career intention tests, personality tests and psychological tests. We have to be careful because in the past this authority – and I don't think it is different from any other authority – has made bad appointments through the inability to interview correctly. Development officers who are the second tier and could become the managers of the future, have a particularly tough time trying to get appointed, but one hopes that in the end we get the right people.

Leisure development officers do certainly play a key role in providing quality service to the residents of an area. They may work in venues such as an ice rink or a sports centre, and need to have a practical knowledge of sports equipment and how to keep plant running as well as supervising events and employees. Because they will promote and implement new initiatives, some personal skills in sport activities are desirable but, above all, someone appointed to one of these important posts would have to show that he or she was mature and principled, for the job entails taking responsibility for staff, customers and financial arrangements.

Leisure centre managers

Leisure centre managers do carry the heaviest burden of responsibility within local authority provision. Apart from dealing with staff and customers, they are also responsible to the chief leisure officer or principal recreation officer who, in turn, implements the policy of the leisure and community services committee of the council, so there is much paper work to be done. In some areas, there will be a general manager who will be helped by deputy managers, assistant managers, managers of specific sites, such as baths and sports stadia, golf-driving ranges, etc., any of whom could on occasions have to deputise for the general manager. It has been a common requirement that applicants for management posts should be 'Innovative and with a good practical knowledge of sports facility operation'. Leadership is also emphasised: 'Ability to lead and motivate a team of multi-disciplinary employees,' and 'Able to supervise and motivate staff.' There are also new requirements creeping in that are signs of changing times such as 'Must be dynamic, commercially minded and committed to ensuring that the leisure centre remains an in-house operation.'

Anyone hoping to come into management nowadays would really need to have taken professional examinations, such as the BTEC National Certificate/Diploma in Leisure Studies, the City and Guilds Certificate for Recreation and Leisure Industry, the Higher National Certificate in Leisure Management, the Diploma of Loughborough Institute of Sport and Recreation Management or a leisure-related university degree like the BSc in Managerial and Administrative Studies. Because the leisure industry has matured so rapidly over the last two decades, increasingly sophisticated and specialised courses have come into being. It is, for instance, possible to take an HNC course in Waterbased Recreation, an HND in Promotions Management, and Masters Degrees in International Tourist Management and Heritage Management. In addition, membership of a professional body, such as the Institute of Leisure and Amenity Management (ILAM); the Institute of Groundsmanship and the Institute of Baths and Recreation Management, is essential, for most of these organisations set their own examinations which are highly regarded and are stepping-stones to promotion.

Commercial clubs for sport and recreation, tennis and fitness, etc., are expanding just as rapidly as the local authority sector, and careful scanning of the press might also reveal opportunities for working in a charitable trust like this one: 'Sports co-ordinator YMCA. High-profile manager capable of leading, controlling, co-ordinating and developing an existing sports and fitness programme.'

Work in sports and recreation offers a most attractive if rather tough career, and to know the business properly it is essential to start on the ground floor and learn by work experience. Leisure management will offer the chance to enter a growing profession with excellent prospects.

Museums and the arts

Those who wish to enter into the world of museums and the arts, will again find that there is a wealth of opportunities, for this is also a rapidly expanding and changing service which is well-funded by central and local government authorities, and at the same time offers prospects in the other sectors. Equality of access and resolve to be active in the field is just as important in this area of leisure as in sport and recreation. For example, this statement of intent precedes all job advertisements published by Walsall Borough Council:

> *Walsall Leisure Services, Museums and Art Galleries*
> We are determined to provide an accessible customer care service to people locally and beyond with varied programmes of exhibitions, events, educational activities and outreach initiatives, encouraging interest and participation for all.

Notices of vacancies emphasize this determination to provide an accessible customer care service, right from the point-of-entry jobs like this one:

> *Museum and Art Gallery. Visitor services assistant.*
> Dealing with a wide range of people on a day to day basis, ensuring their care and comfort and a welcoming environment. Answering enquiries, serving on the sales desk, assisting with security and porterage duties. Candidates should have an interest in the building and its contents and be prepared to work unsocial hours.

A similar, hourly-paid job for part-time attendants at a museum of glass carries much the same duties: 'To include patrolling exhibition galleries, operating sales desk, occasional responsibility for security systems, light cleaning duties, assisting with exhibitions/display. Hours include lunchtime relief and Saturday work plus some evening work. Knowledge of fine and decorative arts preferred but not essential.'

In the other sectors, there is need for guides who are often offered seasonal work at heritage centres and stately homes. The duties 'to welcome, help and provide information for visitors' are basically the same.

The National Trust sometimes has residential posts which are a step up the ladder. Here is an advertisement for such a post: 'House steward. Principal duties include the security, conservation and cleaning of the interiors of this large historic building and assistance with indoor events and functions.' Such posts, whether public or private, generally ask for no more in the way of qualifications than 'Good written English and a genuine interest in museums, galleries, local history and the arts.'

We noted that there were opportunities for graduates to learn managerial skills in sport and recreation, and it is interesting to see that the same sort of opening occurs in the arts divisions of leisure and amenities departments, as this advertisement shows: 'Graduate trainee for operational management in a range of recreational environments including a multi-purpose theatre, leisure and arts centre, swimming pools, entertainments and community facilities, administrative duties, general recreation and arts management.'

For anyone with special skills in, and devotion to, entertainment the following job in a local authority multi-purpose entertainment centre would be a splendid chance to follow an interest and earn a living at the same time. 'Technician. Experience of working within a theatrical environment and with a flair for creativity along with a knowledge of computerized lighting systems and comprehensive sound controls.'

Such a post might lead on to the position of: 'Assistant curator. To supervise the Arts Centre's events and activities. Some assistance with preparation and cleaning required. Most work in the evenings and at weekends.' Note again the need for hands-on work in the cleaning sphere!

The managerial post of curator can also demand some unusual and far-ranging qualities which go far beyond mere desk work: 'Curator: Post with overall responsibility for the day-to-day running of the recently opened heritage centre which is being developed to serve the district, and which comprises a museum, craft workshops, field-training centre and lecture rooms. Outdoor activities may include a pony-trekking station and public refreshment facilities.' For this many-faceted job, candidates are advised that they should possess the Museums Association Diploma while exhibiting 'Professionalism and enthusiasm for customer service' – perhaps experience of working with horses might be an added requirement!

There is perhaps more variety of jobs in the museums and arts division than in leisure centre management. The brief outline of the post of community arts officer, 'To initiate and co-ordinate large-scale art form-focused community arts activities' would baffle anyone who had no experience in that type of work. It would, however, be fully comprehensible to an 'Arts development worker who is based at the museum and art gallery with responsibility for exhibitions and community arts in the area.' The community arts officer would also be assisted by a 'Special projects officer. A permanent member of the Arts and Community Team whose main task will be to develop the Arts in the community strategy with special attention to disadvantaged groups.'

Another borough is seeking an 'Assistant arts officer to assist with the development and promotion of the Arts Festival and to help with the organisation, development and promotion of the Council's Arts policy, which aims to support and develop community arts events and activities throughout the borough.'

Sometimes the official jargon is abandoned in favour of a more direct appeal, as in: 'Wanted! Festival organiser. One year fixed contract to think brilliant thoughts and then make them work for next year's Festival.' There is usually an insistence on equal opportunity, and it is quite common to find interesting and challenging posts such as: 'Co-ordinator Afro-Caribbean and Asian Communities. Involving motivating young black and Asian people and raising the profile of the arts in the community.'

More traditional openings in leisure work also exist, as in: 'Ballroom manager for a purpose-built dance venue used for many types of events from cabaret to disco and special functions. It is equipped with an excellent sound and lighting system and also houses one of the authority's Tourist Information Centres. The work will be varied, dealing with both practical and control sides of the operation on a day-to-day basis including a close liaison with the catering service. Responsible to the entertainments and arts manager, he/she will be expected to develop the present programme of events and increase the public's awareness of the facility. The candidate would be expected to produce evidence of 'Experience of planning and implementing promotional initiatives.'

Outdoor jobs

The idea of getting out and about appeals to many people, and so does the feeling of freedom that comes from working in the open air. For these reasons there is never a shortage of applicants for outdoor jobs in the leisure service. There are certainly some attractive posts being offered, but the time has come for a new breed of worker in the ever popular types of open air job. Consider what Keith Turner, executive co-ordinator of the recently formed Council for Occupational Standards and Qualifications in Environmental Conservation (COSQUEC) has to say about the development of new skills criteria among the 750,000 people employed directly or indirectly in the environmental sector:

Conservation work will, in future, require more than simply an open-necked shirt, a woolly hat and bags of enthusiasm. People will have to show that they have achieved a recognised level of competence and skill to do their jobs. This will apply as much to countryside rangers and leaders of voluntary groups as to directors of archaeological digs and executives of nature conservation trusts.

From 31 March 1992, all qualifications are to be ratified by the National Council for Vocational Qualifications (NCVQ).

The job of litter warden, while not requiring any particular technical skills, does require someone with a friendly nature and a responsible character, and is advertised as being suitable for 'Someone who enjoys working outdoors.' The job is an important link in the chain of conservation work. In an ideal world, no-one would drop or tip litter, but in the real world the fact is that country parks and nature trails would be unsightly and perhaps positively dangerous were it not for the work of the litter warden. Sometimes this type of work is undertaken by a patrol person, whose duties are similar but also include: 'Regular patrol of the park, collection of fishing fees and supervision of fishermen and other park users.' The work of the litter warden is overseen by the countryside ranger, who is usually part of a team which maintains and develops leisure amenities in areas of rural recreation. That such jobs are eagerly sought after is not surprising if one looks at a typical advertisement for a ranger: 'The Country Park is a beautiful 150 acre development on the outskirts of the West Midlands Conurbation offering woodland areas, mapped walking routes, picnic areas, fishing pools, lawned areas, disabled access routes, a visitors' centre and nearby a five-and-a-half-mile linear walk on a disused railway track. The successful applicant must have good communication skills, an ability to work with minimum supervision and who preferably has experience in interpretation, estate management and clerical work. Enthusiasm for outdoor work and aiding preservation of the natural environment is essential, together with the possession of a clean, valid driving licence.' Such posts do offer prospects for promotion as well as an enjoyable way of life, for there exists the post of senior countryside ranger with managerial responsibilities and proportionately higher salary.

In some boroughs similar posts are designated landscape wardens, but a glance at the job description will show that in addition it carries some educational responsibility: 'An outgoing, suitably experienced person with the confidence and ability required to deal with the public at all levels, including involvement with school parties and other visiting groups; an understanding of nature conservation principles and practice plus a wide range of practical skills necessary. You will be responsible to the senior warden for the

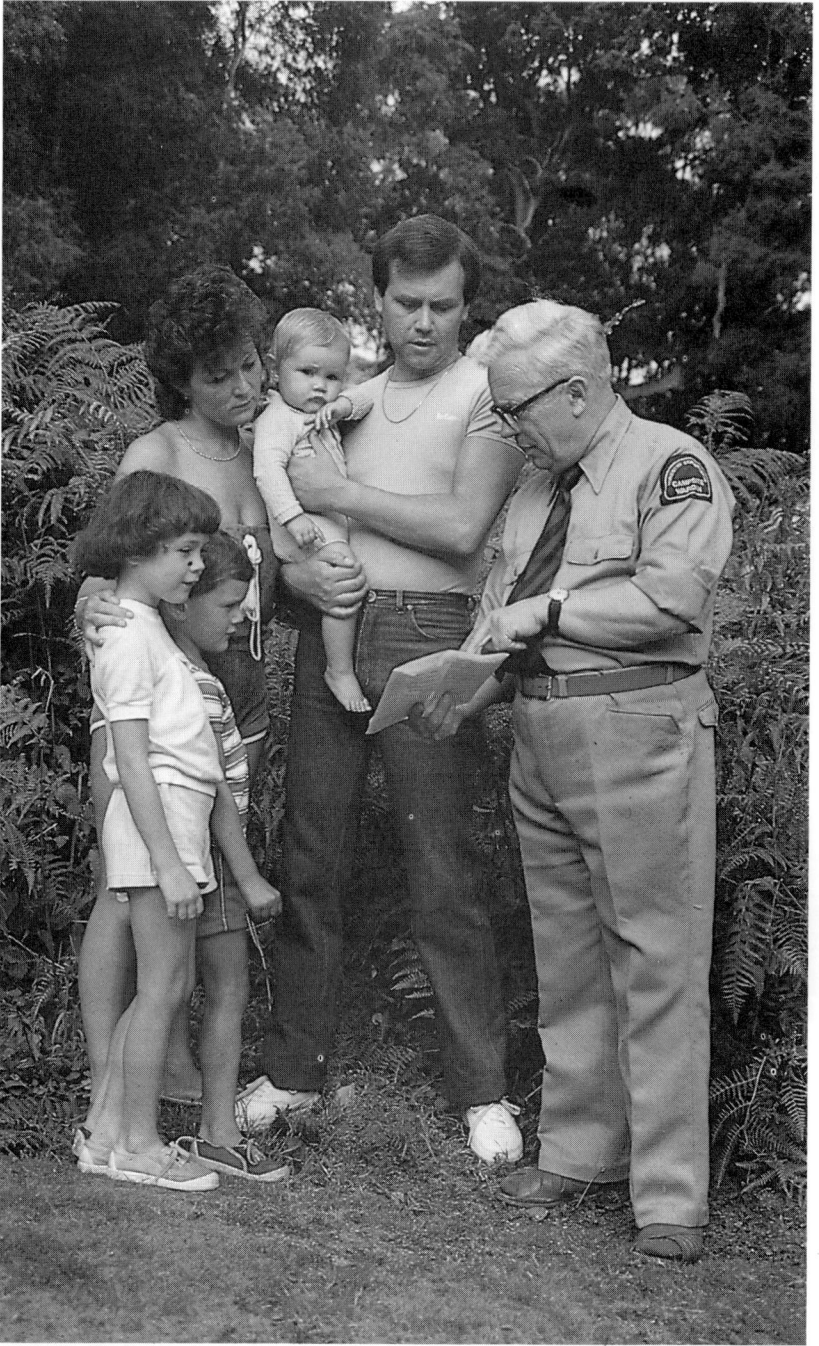

An interesting and varied job is that of a Forestry Commission Warden.

(Courtesy of the Forestry Commission.)

day-to-day running of the reserve. Wardening of this reserve requires shift working during the summer and at weekends/bank holidays throughout the year.'

The National Parks, Country Parks and areas of great natural beauty all have visitor centres which have shops and serve refreshments, so an important member of staff would be the visitor service attendant, who would typically be: 'Based at the Country Park. Duties include souvenir shop sales and other visitor services. The ability to perform crafts would be an advantage.'

We must remember also that there are, in both the public and the private sectors, enterprises such as: Historic Working Farm ('demonstrates life on an upland farm before the introduction of the internal combustion engine . . . farming and craft demonstrations'),

- The Rare Breed Collection (here the past lives and breathes in a heritage of many rare and ancient breeds of farm animal'),
- The Shire Horse Centre ('dray rides; mare and foal; farrier; bygones'),
- Heron Corn Mills ('a fascinating eighteenth-century water-powered corn mill, restored to full working order. Friendly staff will happily explain and demonstrate the mill's features and provide you with a real insight into the past').

Many other examples could be cited, but the point is that the educational and recreational aspect of country life is now an

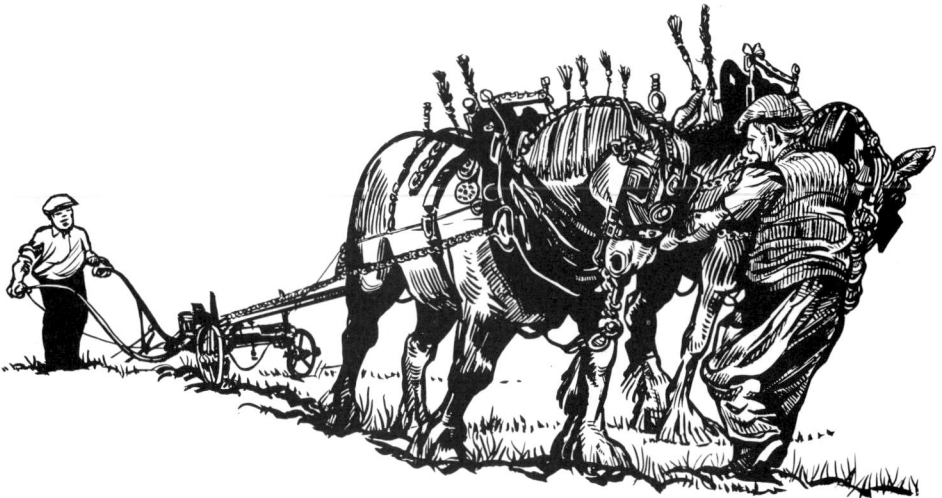

If you have patience, a love of animals and a fondness for the open air, a job at an historic working farm might suit you ideally.

important part of the leisure industry, and creates many jobs, as is seen by this vacancy for a farm manager. 'The Country Park is being developed as a major outdoor leisure facility. This includes working farm visitor centres open to school visits and the general public. A vacancy exists for a farm manager.'

There would be little point in telling the public about beautiful and historic countryside if they did not know where they could walk freely, so many rural councils appoint a 'Rights-of-way officer (to be attached to the Leisure Services Countryside Unit). The successful candidate will play a key role in bringing the Council's Definitive Map of Public Rights of Way up to date, and be expected to discuss changes to the Public Path Network with Parish Councils, land-owners and members of the public in general.' This officer would be responsible to the countryside project officer, whose job involves 'Working with the voluntary sector on a range of initiatives in the county's countryside. The postholder will play a key role in identify-ing potential for further improving access to public rights of way and particularly to steer the new long-distance bridleway to completion; will also take responsibility for managing the authority's new voluntary ranger service.' The words 'new' and 'innovative' appear again and again in this type of advertisement, and show how rapidly things are changing in the countryside as leisure provision extends. The National Rivers Authority (NRA), for instance, is seeking a conservation and recreation officer 'to assist in the promotion of new initiatives and the management of existing sites'.

Of course, beautifying the environment and providing open spaces for the public to relax in is not a new thing for the leisure and recreation departments of councils; it was, as we have noted, one of their earliest powers back in the nineteenth century, and there is a long tradition of skilled and dedicated horticultural work in local government. These jobs still exist, but now there is more emphasis on scientific knowledge and ongoing educational initiatives. Entrants to the Parks and Open Spaces Section of the Leisure Department of one district council now begin as horticultural trainees. 'We are offering training places on the Parks Horticultural two-year training programme. The scheme is open to all 16 year old school leavers who are interested in horticulture and willing to learn.' That there are prospects in this type of work is shown by a district council's vacancy for a 'Technical Assistant (Parks and Open Spaces department). This post creates an excellent career opportun-ity for an enthusiastic person suitably qualified or experienced in grounds maintenance management and horticultural work. The post reports directly to the Senior Technician Officer (Horticulture). The successful applicant should have formal horticultural and arboricultural training, with experience of, or a willingness to learn a computer-based management of contracts system'.

Horticultural Officers themselves can specialise, and a district council is looking for one 'To develop and maintain an effective arboricultural service to the Leisure Services and other Council Departments. Must have knowledge of current arboricultural practice and techniques plus the ability to promote awareness of the value of trees.' Positions with local councils are well-paid and stable, but it is worth remembering that for every such job vacancy there will be five or six times as many in various garden centres, garden worlds, garden kingdoms, etc.

It should be borne in mind that outdoor jobs also include sports centres and adventure holiday centres. A local authority for instance is advertising for a stadium and sports manager. 'For the management and maintenance of a Sports Stadium providing track and field facilities to national standards for the use of clubs, schools and the general public.'

A registered educational charity is seeking a head of outdoor education centre (Outdoor Pursuits Field Centre) 'To lead the Centre into a new phase of its development and to market and manage its commercial activities.' An attractive position, but one that demands 'High personal competence in rock-climbing and other outdoor activities,' which rather narrows down the field of applicants!

Working in the open air, enjoying natural surroundings and doing a worthwhile service for the environment is an enviable way of earning a living, but just in case the emphasis on official posts and career prospects seems exclusively mercenary, let us consider what Jenny Baker, national volunteers manager of the National Trust has to say:

> Volunteers of all ages and from all backgrounds help the National Trust in over a hundred different ways. We have bakers and botanists, entomologists and mill minders, pilots and architects giving us their support and services for nothing. We value the enthusiasm and expertise of our volunteers – they show their support of the Trust in a very active and practical way.

It is worth stressing at this point that the remarks of the COSQUEC co-ordinator quoted above refer to 'professional, paid' conservationists. The National Trust estimates that nearly 20,000 volunteers gave 1.1 million hours of service to the Trust in 1990, helping it to complete tasks it would not otherwise be able to afford.

Tourism, promotion and sales

Careers in tourism, promotion and sales are very rewarding in every sense, and are part of a growing market. The English Tourist Board

(ETB) estimates that more than two million jobs in Britain are supported by tourism and leisure. About 160,000 new jobs were created between 1985 and 1989, making it one of the fastest growing areas of the economy, and one person in 10 is now employed directly in tourism and leisure or in related jobs.

While we are quoting figures, though, there is a sad statistic to note. According to a 1991 report from the Tourism and Leisure Industries Sector Group of the National Economic Development Council (NEDC), fewer than 10 per cent of British tourism and leisure managers have the relevant qualifications to do their jobs, and even fewer take advantage of in-post training programmes. Sir Brian Wolfson, chairman of the NEDC's Tourism and Leisure Industries Sector Group, expressed concern about this situation:

We have to ensure that enthusiastic and qualified people come into the industry and want to continue improving their management skills. It is a common dream to open a restaurant or run a hotel with enthusiasm as the only qualification.

William Davis, chairman of the British Tourist Authority (BTA) did admit that careers in tourism had, at times, a poor image:

Skills training often has little penetration outside major companies. We must show people, including the unemployed, that this is an attractive business to be in. It is vital that the tourism industry is led by professional managers.

It is not surprising, then, to see an advertisement for a tourist information centres manager 'for the management and operation of the five tourist information centres within the County network'. It is interesting that in addition to the normal stipulation that the applicant should possess a BTEC certificate/diploma or equivalent, it is stated that 'An ability to converse and/or write in a language other than English will be an advantage.' So this authority at least is looking towards the coming battle for customers which will follow the opening of the Channel Tunnel. All leisure professionals should try to make themselves aware of the impact of the single market in Europe and of Britain's fuller integration into Europe.

Most leisure and recreation departments have a marketing and promotions officer 'for marketing and promoting leisure and community facilities and services'. He or she is required to be 'enthusiastic and imaginative'. For this post, two years' experience in the field is required, and a useful way of putting in that rather specialised service is to have been a publicity and promotions co-ordinator 'providing learning opportunities for young people to gain publicity experience producing publicity material, forming networks with the local press, monitoring, researching and main-taining the impact of publicity methods'. This job, we are told with commendable honesty, requires someone with 'amazing powers of tact, organisation, stamina and vitality – not a post for the faint-hearted'. Another council advertises for a press officer 'with knowledge of local, regional and national press plus the ability to develop contacts and stories'.

For those with a sports skill, there are jobs in demonstrating and selling. First-class companies which supply ski equipment sometimes offer posts which combine knowledge, experience and enjoyment by means of an advertisement like this: 'We are the fastest growing sports retailer in the UK, and are currently looking for an experienced ski technician to join our team. Knowledge of skis, boots, clothing, etc., is essential in order to provide expert advice to our customers. Full training in systems, etc., will be given.' If fairways and greens are your speciality, you might be interested in a vacancy for a golf shop manager, 'Required to manage new store

Working in the leisure industry can be a rewarding career, especially if you have the personality to persuade users of all ages to take up adventurous new pursuits.

(Photograph Dave Wallace.)

assisting in general sales of golf clubs and accessories to the public. Must have product knowledge and interest in customer needs. Age 21+; own transport required.' In the same vein, an opportunity for a receptionist and sales person at a golf and squash club offers independence and a good wage, stipulating that: 'You will be required to work unsupervised in a busy reception area, having responsibility for an electronic cash till, telephone and associated systems. Other duties include dealing with customers in a courteous and effective manner, stock control of goods and refreshments, maintaining good order and responsibility for the security of the premises.'

Some educational experiences can be combined with career building, as in this case: 'Walt Disney World' Fellowship. A unique opportunity to learn and work for one year at Walt Disney World, Orlando, Florida. You will take part in a special management training programme and work in the 'Magic of Wales' gift shop in the United Kingdom pavilion, Epcot Centre. The Fellowship runs for twelve months and is an ideal chance for a young person wishing to develop a career in leisure and tourism.'

Even the voluntary sector offers the chance to be entrepreneurial and sell membership on a paid basis, as this advertisement shows: 'New member recruiter. A part-time new member recruiter is required to work at Powis Castle, a National Trust property, from Easter to the end of October.'

We have looked at career opportunities in the leisure field, but we have only skimmed the surface. There are many jobs that we have not even touched upon, but by studying the national papers, your local press, the professional leisure journals and magazines, you will gain a fuller impression of all the openings for a career which combines service and security and makes studying for a leisure qualification well worth while.

Conclusion

We have asked a few searching questions about the leisure industry, and have come up with some answers and several heartening examples of good practice. The topic is so wide that no single book can cover it all, but it is hoped that by offering this overview we might have stimulated new interest and heightened awareness.

Leisure provision and the philosophy that goes with it are constantly changing. It is a dynamic area full of ideas and objectives that vary from place to place and year to year, but the greatest challenge which is facing providers of leisure facilities is how to resolve the conflict between preserving the natural environment, and supplying the recreational needs of people. We must ensure conservation and encourage wildlife, while also trying to meet the demands of all the community.

Whether your interest is in becoming a paid employee, an active volunteer worker or simply studying the subject for pleasure, it is hoped that you will continue reading and observing in order to play your part in making people's lives happier and healthier as well as reducing environmental waste and vandalism of all kinds – after all, *our* environment begins in the places where we live and work.

INDEX